1. 95

Customer Care

The personnel implications

Incomes Data Services
Institute Of Personnel Management

October 1989

CONTENTS

First Published 1989
© Incomes Data Services/Institute of Personnel Management

Produced by Incomes Data Services, 193 St John Street, London EC1V 4LS and printed by Dotesios Printers Ltd, Trowbridge, Wiltshire.
ISBN O 85292 428 3

ACKNOWLEDGEMENTS

We would like to thank all the organisations which provided information so willingly for this publication. In particular we would like to thank the following case study organisations:

Arun District Council
Braintree District Council
Birmingham City Council
Gloucestershire County Council
London Borough of Camden
Teignbridge District Council
Wrekin District Council

Belfast City Hospital
Liverpool District Health Authority
Pembrokeshire District Health Authority
Peterborough District Health Authority
Trent Regional Health Authority
West Dorset District Health Authority

British Rail
London Underground Ltd
Northern Ireland Department of
    Economic Development
Northern Ireland Electricity
Royal Mail Letters - Glasgow District
Stroud College of Further Education

British Airways
British Telecom
MBS Services Ltd

Several other organisations provided us with material but wished to remain anonymous.

IDS PUBLIC SECTOR UNIT

OUR RANGES OF SERVICES

PUBLIC SERVICE DIGEST is published monthly and brings you both news and features on the latest developments within the public sector. Our service covers all those working in the public's service, by they in central government, the NHS, local government, the public corporations or those in voluntary organisations. Each month, the Digest provides details of the latest pay and conditions agreements at national level, bargaining developments, competitive tendering initiatives, recruitment and retention measures, performance related pay and merit bonus schemes, relocation packages, new flexible working arrangements, training programmes and employment planning. In short, all the issues facing local personnel managers and trade union negotiators within the public sector.

SPECIAL PUBLICATIONS are issued separately at regular intervals. These cover major areas of interest and new developments. Examples include Competitive Tendering in the Public Sector, Salaries and Benefits in Local Government, Paying For Performance in the Public Sector and a Guide to Performance-Related Pay. Each year we also publish a major review of public sector pay which summarises the latest developments and looks at prospects for the coming year.

CONTRACT RESEARCH is also available for those subscribers with specific requirements for information. IDS has unique archive of information on the public sector which we use as the base to carry out complete research projects on a fee-paying basis. The unit has carried out assignments for the Government, public sector employers, trade unions, the Institute of Personnel Management, professional associations, management consultants and the media. If you require rapid, accurate research in public sector employee relations, the IDS Public Sector Unit is at your service. Further details from IDS, 193 St John Street, London EC1V 4LS (Tel: 01-250 3434).

INTRODUCTION

The last decade has seen an increasing interest in customer care and 'total quality management'. While most of this has been in the private sector, in both manufacturing and service industries, competitive and financial pressures have led to these ideas spreading to the public sector. Much of the private sector theory and experience is valuable to all types of organisations but it is clearly the case that direct transfer of some of the private sector's methods to the public sector is not easy.

Not only are the public services (central government departments, the NHS, local government and education) under the control of political masters who are ultimately answerable to the public through the electoral system, but the concept of a 'customer' has much wider connotations than is the case with a private company.

DEFINING CUSTOMER CARE

For the purpose of this publication we interpret 'customer care' as meaning any strategy designed to improve the quality of services to the public. Consumers of public services form a wide-ranging group - it includes recipients of social security benefits; tax payers; companies seeking advice or customs clearance; patients; users of local council leisure facilities; users of public transport; council house tenants; ratepayers; road users; children, the elderly and the physically and mentally disabled in council care; people on probation; users of the social services; pupils and students in the education services; etc. The list is almost endless.

This myriad collection of service users or 'clients' illustrates the problem of trying to define the 'customer' in the public services; by comparison, the definition in the private sector is generally much easier to formulate.

OUR RESEARCH PROJECT

So how do public sector organisations define their 'customers'? How do they find out what they want from services? How can services be improved? How many of the private sector's management techniques are appropriate to the public sector? What part can employees play in creating the strategies to improve services? How can employees be motivated to provide better services? What role does the personnel department have in all this?

To answer these questions, the Public Sector Standing Committee of the IPM, in conjunction with the IDS Public Sector Unit, undertook a research project; this involved case study interviews with 24 organisations, along with a review of the published literature. This exercise took place over some six months and included visits to both public and private sector organisations. The results are now published in this special IDS/IPM report.

This report does not tell organisations how to improve customer care, they must decide this for themselves; instead it provides an overview of the subject for those starting out on this track or reviewing their existing strategies. The report identifies the philosophical and theoretical origins of 'customer care', examines the current debate on how such strategies can work in the public sector, and looks at what methods are available; most importantly, it reviews how the personnel function plays its role within these wider strategies.

OUR CONCLUSIONS

In general, our research suggests that, while the public sector has much to learn from the private sector, a number of major differences between the two sectors makes the direct transfer of many of the private sector strategies difficult. For example, the huge variety of 'customers' in the public sector, some of whom may be uncooperative and even hostile, and the absence of profits from which to fund improvements, create very different circumstances to those facing private companies. An increase in 'business' may be the last thing a social services department or a hospital, for example, may want.

Moreover, the public services were built on the ethic of public service rather than cost efficiency. This has changed somewhat over the past few years as Government financial and legislative pressures have encouraged public sector bodies to provide 'value for money'. Many organisations say that, though painful, these pressures have had benefits in reducing unnecessary bureaucracy and cutting out waste. However, there is now increasing pressure to provide quality as well as cost efficiency. This is perhaps a reflection of the change in public attitudes. There is an increasing recognition that 'cheapest' is not always best - especially because public concern about the environment, public transport, public safety, the health service and education (if opinion polls are to be believed) appears to be increasing.

Changing The Logo Not Enough

Several of the organisations we visited stressed that customer care was not just about changing the organisation's logo, repainting the vehicles in new colours or uprating the staff suggestion scheme. Real improvements can only be achieved if there is a comprehensive review of the quality of services provided and a wide-ranging strategy to make radical changes.

A central aspect of any review must be the involvement of employees in not just making suggestions for improvements but in the formulation of the strategies to improve services. In most cases there is a fund of knowledge among employees just waiting to be tapped. The father of 'total quality management', W. Edwards Deming, maintains that the vast majority of failures in quality are due to management, rather than the workforce. If the systems are badly designed, employees can do no more.

The Personnel Role

For this reason the role of the personnel manager is crucial to any strategy to improve service quality. It is the duty of personnel to assist line managers in devising 'customer care' projects so that the all important contribution of employees is considered. In the public sector in particular, where both collective bargaining and trade unionism are strong traditions, the role of personnel in easing the transition to a new, 'quality' approach is vital. For many public sector employees, 'customer care' strategies may be seen simply as 'more work for the same money' - again, public sector managers, limited in their ability to improve pay and benefits for often low-paid staff, have a major exercise on their hands if these projects are to work.

It is the aim of this publication to provide a starting point for these personnel staff. A companion book on 'Total Quality, Success Through People' by Ron Collard, published by the IPM, provides more information on private sector techniques. The present publication concentrates on the public sector's experiences, but contains a number of private sector examples and gives general advice on 'customer care' methods. The ways in which public service organisations have attempted to improve customer care, in spite of the limitations placed on them, which we discuss above, should make useful reading for all personnel managers, be they in the private or public sectors.

Our Steering Committee

This publication has been jointly produced by the Institute of Personnel Management's Public Sector Standing Committee and the Public Sector Unit of Incomes Data Services. The steering committee in charge of the research project for this book included:

John Train, Personnel Manager, British Gas Scotland, Chairman PSSC

Terry Collin, Senior Lecturer, Suffolk College of Higher Education

Peter Dooks, Principal Administrative Officer (non-teaching staff), Cleveland County Council

Campbell Ford, ACAS

Alastair Killen, Civil Service Commission, Northern Ireland

Paul Thain, Director of Personnel, Norwich Health Authority

Geoff White, Managing Editor, IDS Research

Dianah Worman, Secretary of the PSSC

In addition to the advice and guidance given by these individuals regarding the development of the project, thanks are given to the researchers, Matthew Bell and Sheila Cohen of the IDS Public Sector Unit, who undertook the research and wrote much of the material included in this publication.

Chapter 1

THE GROWTH OF CUSTOMER CARE

A major development over the past decade has been the increasing concern for quality in goods and services. In the private sector this concern has been the product of intense international competition for markets following the recession in the early 1980s. In particular, it is a by-product of the growing penetration of American and European markets by Japanese manufacturers, who are renowned for their emphasis on quality.

In the public sector the emphasis on the quality of service is more recent and the main reasons have been: 1) the increasing influence of private sector management methods; 2) mounting pressures of a series of legislative measures and reductions in financial resources; and 3) a response by some local councils to compulsory competitive tendering which emphasises the 'quality' rather than the 'cost' of services.

In this chapter we look at:

* Quality In The Private Sector

* Quality In The Public Sector

* Legislation In The Public Sector

* Public Services - The Political Response

* What Is 'Customer Care' All About?

* Involving The Workforce

QUALITY IN THE PRIVATE SECTOR

The emergence of 'customer care' in the private sector can be traced back to the writings of some influential management theorists, such as William Edwards Deming, J.M. Juran, and Philip Crosby. 'Total quality' management techniques are discussed in more detail in a new book by Ron Collard ('Total Quality', IPM 1989). In this chapter we summarise the main influences.

W. Edwards Deming

The campaign to promote quality within industry began in 1950 with a lecture given in Japan by Deming, an American, at the invitation of the Union of Japanese Scientists and Engineers. Deming's view overturned the opinion in the post-war period that improving quality added to costs. He said that

1

improving quality could, 1) lead to improved productivity which reduced costs, 2) enable prices to be reduced and, (3) increase market share.

Deming went on to take his message to the chief executives of Japan's twenty-one biggest corporations, and by 1951 he had convinced 500 top managers of the importance of quality. Japanese industry has now instituted the Deming Award for outstanding achievement in quality improvement and Deming's philosophy has now been adopted in his own country by a wide range of companies including Ford, General Motors and the Nashua Corporation.

British companies are now taking up much of Deming's philosophy of 'Total Quality Management'. A recent conference on the subject, promoted by the Industrial Society, featured speakers from British Telecom and Avon Cosmetics, as well as ex-managers from Rank Xerox and Hewlett Packard who have now become consultants in this field.

J. M. Juran

J. M. Juran is a close associate of Deming and has worked with him since the 1940s. Juran emphasises the responsibility of management for quality, arguing that at least 85 per cent of the failures in any organisation are the responsibility of management. In a conventional management system, the assumption is often made that the level of performance cannot be improved and that the reasons for this lie largely with the workforce. What Juran terms 'managerial breakthrough' occurs when the managerial attitude changes to one of believing that the level of performance can be improved. Juran argues that the means of improvement is the manager's responsibility.

Juran also emphasises the long-term nature of quality improvement (in some Japanese organisations this has spanned a period of twenty years) and he urges an end to the short-term, 'fire-fighting' perspective still common among employers.

Philip Crosby

A third, more recent source of ideas on quality has been the influential series of books published by Philip Crosby, notably 'Quality Is Free' (McGraw Hill, 1978); these books have been used as the basis for British Telecom's Total Quality Management programme. Crosby places his central emphasis on 'dealing with people'. Crosby believes that five factors govern quality management:

- quality means conformance, not elegance;

- there is no such thing as a quality problem;

- there is no such thing as the economics of quality - it is always cheaper to do the job right first time;

- the only performance measurement is the cost of quality; and

- the only performance standard is zero defects.

(Quoted from Collard, 'Total Quality' IPM, 1989).

The message of all three theorists is that quality, above all, depends on attitude.

Peters And Waterman

A further influence has been the work of Tom Peters and Bob Waterman, authors of 'In Search Of Excellence' (Harper & Row, 1982). Their view is that 'the excellent companies really are close to their customers. That's it. Other companies talk about it; the excellent companies do it'. More recently, another book co-authored by Peters, argues that 'exceptional' care of the customer is the only way to create and sustain superior performance in the private or public sector (T. Peters and N. Austin, 'A Passion For Excellence: The Leadership Difference' Fontana 1985).

QUALITY IN THE PUBLIC SECTOR

The ideas contained in the book, 'In Search Of Excellence', are now being increasingly promoted in the public sector. The authors of an article in 'Local Government Studies' (Hancox, Worrall And Pay in 'Local Government Studies', 1989),looking at the experiences of Wrekin Council, say that the stimulus for Wrekin's customer care policy came in part from Peters and Waterman. Like many other public sector organisations, they identify commitment to these ideas from the top as a central factor. They point to 'the need for a clear and strong commitment from senior management and members because, like all initiatives in organisations, it must have its 'champions' who will enthuse the organisation with their drive and commitment'.

Many of the ideas central to customer care initiatives are now embodied in an influential publication of the Local Government Training Board, 'Getting Closer To The Public'. A similar stimulus within the Health Service was the 1983 Griffiths Report, which generated widespread interest in patient satisfaction and 'quality assurance'. It also encouraged managers to conduct surveys of patient satisfaction. More recently, patient participation groups have been introduced, as suggested in the 1986 DHSS Green Paper on primary health care.

The authors of 'Getting Closer To The Public', John Stewart and Michael Clarke, criticise local authorities for seeing themselves as providing services to the public, rather than for the public. They urge those providing local authority services to drop the assumption that they know what is best for the customer, and to focus instead on the customer's changing needs and wants.

3

Local authority staff who are encouraged to see their role from the customer's perspective will ask themselves not 'how can the authority continue to provide this or that service' but 'how can the authority best meet the public's changing needs?'.

'Getting Closer To The Public', which was produced in 1987 as a summary of a number of previous LGTB papers on the subject, symbolises a growing drive within the public sector to defend and to promote its role in providing satisfactory public services.

Pressures On Resources

This role has been increasingly challenged in two ways: firstly through pressure on financial resources, accompanied by privatisation and, secondly, through legislation which has made some fundamental changes to the public sector.

Within local government, considerable strain has been caused by the gradual reduction of the central government Rate Support Grant. A number of councils have been ratecapped, which has limited the amount of revenue they can raise locally. Health authority income has also been affected by the proposals of the Reallocation of Resources Working Party (RAWP), which were designed to give more money to authorities outside the metropolitan areas at the expense of metropolitan authorities, while the 1989 NHS White Paper, 'Working For Patients', suggests a programme for 'opting out' by which hospitals would become independent trusts. General Practitioners' budgets would also be subject to restraint.

In the five years since 1984 a number of major public sector organisations have been privatised, including British Telecom (1984) and British Airways (1987); and the electricity industry is being organised for privatisation in 1990. These developments have created a competitive environment which in many cases has led public sector organisations to review the quality of their services.

LEGISLATION IN THE PUBLIC SECTOR

A comparable process to privatisation is taking place within the public services, namely, compulsory competitive tendering; this has been encouraged by the Government by the use of circulars, as in the NHS, and by specific legislation, the most obvious example of which is the Local Government Act 1988, which requires local authorities to put a set group of 'defined' services out to tender according to a prescribed timetable. The services currently affected are in 'direct service' areas such as refuse collection, street cleaning and building (itself affected by the Local Government Planning and Land Act of 1980 which put restrictions on council direct labour building organisations).

The need for councils to cost their services and to draw up detailed specifications in the run up to competitive tendering clearly affects their assessments of their services. It also has repercussions on the quality of the support services, leading to the setting up of departmental cost centres and 'Service Level Agreements'.

Other laws have had, or are likely to have, a considerable impact on services:

- The Housing Act 1988 introduced the 'pick-a-landlord' scheme where by tenants can choose a landlord other than their local council. The Act also proposes setting up Housing Action Trusts which will take over council estates.

- The Education Reform Act 1988 introduced among other things a timetable for the Local Management of Schools from 1990, removing direct control from local education authorities (currently managed by County Councils). The Government has also abolished the Inner London Education Authority and devolved the management of schools in the area to the London boroughs.

- The Poll Tax or Community Charge will change and in some cases reduce the basis of local government income, as well as imposing an administrative burden on councils in collecting the tax.

These measures, along with the 1989 NHS White Paper, 'Working For Patients', and other developments in the Civil Service, have combined to promote an environment of decentralised financial management and competition which has put many public sector organisations under considerable pressure to re-examine and streamline their services.

'Value For Money'

The result in many cases, however, has been a positive response in which financial stringency has led organisations to re-examine the role of services and to direct them more effectively towards the needs of the customer. Liverpool Health Authority, for example, was faced with a reduction of its resources under the RAWP proposals. Its response was to draw up an Acute Services Strategy based on a reduction of the number of hospital sites within the authority and the bringing together of services in 'centres of excellence'. In this way the authority's services have been improved as a direct result of the need to become more efficient.

Some local authorities have also responded to financial reductions by adopting more commercial strategies, regarding these as ways of safeguarding ratepayers' interests. Braintree District Council, for example, adopted the slogan "Braintree Means Business" as part of a market-orientated strategy centred on the encouragement of investment in small industrial units. Along the same lines, Arun District Council began its moves towards customer care with a major restructuring aimed at increasing

5

financial independence and responsibility at the point of contact with the public.

Cost Centres

Almost all the local authorities and the other public sector organisations we have studied have gone some way along the road towards the decentralisation and separation of financially independent units within the organisation. Camden Council, for example, despite its opposition to the Government's competitive tendering legislation, is now moving towards setting up sections, such as its residential homes, as independent cost centres. The authority is introducing 'Service Level Agreements', which require all departments to cost services to one another on a commercial 'contractor-client' basis.

The same trend can be seen in education, where Local Financial Management is being introduced from 1990. Stroud College of Further Education, for example, where survival depends on the number of students, has adopted a market-led strategy, with course units run as independent cost centres. Other public sector organisations covered in our research have reorganised on a similar basis of cost centres and business plans.

PUBLIC SERVICES - THE POLITICAL RESPONSE

The changes outlined above represent a necessary response by public sector organisations, whatever their political views, to the financial restrictions imposed on them. Competition, Government legislation and reductions in public spending have led to a 'streamlining' of services and more attention to efficiency. These, in turn, have led to a greater emphasis on the needs of the consumer. Some organisations however, have responded with a political defence of public services; they emphasise the role of the public sector in serving the community, while acknowledging that some providers of public services have, until now, been lacking in their awareness of the consumer.

The Three 'C's' Versus The Three 'E's'

This 'value for money' approach to customer care has its roots in the Audit Commission's well-known definition of improved services in terms of the 'three E's' - Efficiency, Effectiveness and Economy. A number of public sector organisations,however, have begun to challenge this view; in contrast to the 'three E's', Gloucestershire County Council, for example, suggests counterposing the 'three C's' - Competent, Caring and Competitive.

Along similar lines, Camden Council argues that it has always shown a concern for the consumer through its overall community orientation, which it sees as representative of Labour-led authorities. Lewisham Borough Council representatives also make the point that their concern for the needs of community-based groups and organisations pre-dates the more market-led approach to consumer care, promoted strongly by the Audit Commission, and other government pressures towards competition and privatisation.

An Opportunity, Not A Threat

This defence of public services is based on the argument that the private sector would be incapable of providing as high a level of service to the community. As a Camden Council representative put it, referring to employees working in their own time to repair the 1987 hurricane damage: 'Having your own DLO means you get a response - you can't put a price on that'.

However, it is also acknowledged that public services have often suffered from bureaucracy, inflexibility and a lack of awareness of the consumer. In response to this a number of organisations have produced statements which show that they regard the current competitive tendering legislation as less of a threat and more of an opportunity to improve services radically and to demonstrate the special value of the public sector. The Labour-controlled Association of Metropolitan Authorities, for example, in its guide to competitive tendering entitled 'Don't Panic', comments:

'The preparations for competitive tendering will provide authorities with an opportunity to look in detail at their services. There will be a chance to re-assess whether they are really meeting community needs and then make appropriate changes and improvements. Imaginative councils supported by effective management and unions will see these proposals as a chance to prove the value of publicly run services'.

The Labour Party's 'Quality Street'

This kind of approach to improving and defending public services is summed up in the Labour Party's recent proposals, presented in the final draft of its Policy Review. Based on its 'Quality Street' draft programme for local government, the Policy Review section on 'Consumers and the Community' declares that Labour's intention is to set up a Quality Commission responsible for promoting the quality of local government services (even when these are provided by the private sector). Similar commissions would be set up for health and education. A Labour government would also place legal requirements on councils to set and publicise targets and standards for each service, through a system of 'service contracts'. Labour would also establish local quality audits which would widen the accountancy-based methods used by the Audit Commission to include local managers, professionals and consumer representatives.

WHAT IS CUSTOMER CARE ALL ABOUT?

In the public sector, there is no 'production line', and until recently the whole concept of 'the customer' as a description of service users was foreign, or at least novel, to many providers of services. So how do we define the role of the 'customer' within the public sector in a way which can usefully connect with the nature of public sector services?

Consumerism And The Public Sector

It is often seen as more appropriate to refer to users of public sector services as consumers rather than customers, since customer implies direct purchase of a commodity or service. The concept of the consumer is of recent origin, stemming from the launch in 1957 of the Consumers' Association, whose publication 'Which?' is now supported by 750,000 subscribers. But the concept of the consumer represented by 'Which?' and the Consumers' Association is mainly centred on the rights of individual purchasers of goods.

The National Consumer Council (NCC) was set up by a Labour Government in 1975 to represent the interests of consumers to public bodies, including central government, local government and the nationalised industries. In this way the consumer approach was carried forward to develop a more collective, public sector-orientated view of consumer rights. There are now said to be two definitions of consumerism - 'the narrow and fairly familiar meaning used to describe problems associated with the consumption of 'high street' goods and services; and the broader usage applied to problems associated with the use of public services' (Hambleton, "Consumerism, Decentralisation, Democracy",in Public Administration, Summer 1988).

The National Consumer Council has continued to promote the broader definition, with publications that set out to provide consumer criteria for evaluating public services, such as 'Measuring Up' (1986) which was based on the contrast between 'what does the service do?' and 'what is it supposed to do?' The NCC holds an annual Congress at which community representatives such as tenants' organisations, as well as professional advice workers, gather to discuss a collective response to consumer provision in the public sector.

This emphasis on the need for consumer monitoring of services on a collective or community basis is echoed in the 1988 draft of the Labour Party's Policy Review on 'Consumer and the Community', which argues that the two 'cannot be separated'.

Greater Wealth, Greater Choice

At the same time, however, consumer concern within the public sector has been based to some extent on the argument that improved material conditions in some areas of society have provided consumers with a degree of choice not previously available to them. A Fabian pamphlet, 'Socialism, Merit and Efficiency', argues strongly that 'Wealth allows choice, and thus comparison...It is the enemy of blanket collective provision'. It claims that 'when there was not such wealth among the very large majority, collective provision, for all its uniformity, brusqueness and remoteness, was not only tolerated but often welcomed'.

The need to promote consumer interests within the public sector is therefore associated with the need for organisations like local authorities and the NHS to promote a more modern image that recognises consumers as discerning individuals prepared to take their custom elsewhere, a fact that has been acknowledged by many such organisations. Arun District Council, for example, located in an affluent coastal resort on the south coast with a high proportion of elderly residents, is aware that its community care services may be rivalled or overtaken by private sector provision. Belfast City Hospital believes that there has been a change in the way the public perceives the health service, and that people now expect to receive higher standards of service and treatment.

The Five Principles

Given this increasing degree of consumer discernment and choice, many public bodies are adopting the five 'tenets of consumerism' which have been identified by consumer groups. These are, says Martin Smith, author of a Fabian pamphlet on this topic (Fabian pamphlet No. 513), related to a 'more dynamic' definition of consumerism as 'the organised expression of the aspirations of the consumers and users of goods and services for greater control over their immediate environment'. As such, they are perhaps even more relevant to the public sector, where consumers tend to press for their rights in groups (such as tenants). The five principles are:

- **Access** This can be looked at in two ways: ease in obtaining desired goods or services, and accessibility to public organisations. Both may be limited by poverty, ignorance or disability. Many councils, for example, are bringing in measures to increase public access by opening up council meetings, committees, etc.

- **Choice** Real choice assumes unrestricted access, but in the case of public services, individual choices cannot often be directly translated into action, and performance standards such as those suggested in the NCC's 'Measuring Up' have to be used to ensure that the widest range of consumer preferences are integrated into public services. Consumer surveys are another way of ensuring this (see Chapter 2).

- **Information** Clearly, access to full and reliable information on public services is closely linked to customer choice. Many public sector organisations are now concentrating on increasing their flow of information to the public.

- **Redress** This is a crucial area of consumer rights. Consumers now have considerable rights of redress, or of compensation, in the private sector, but the picture is 'more complex and less satisfactory', says Smith, when it comes to public service delivery. A report on complaints procedures in local government produced by the University of Sheffield in 1987 showed that less than half the authorities surveyed had procedures for handling complaints, and of these only a small proportion gave any publicity to their them.

- **Representation** In principle, this means that the interests of consumers should be represented to decision-makers at all points in the system; in practice, it is difficult to implement within the public sector. This is partly because a political system for representation already exists in the case of local government, and partly because a lack of resources in other areas makes consumer representation ineffectual. In the NHS, for example, Community Health Councils are supposed to represent the interests of consumers, but, according to Jenny Potter, author of 'Consumerism and the Public Sector' (Public Administration Summer 1988), 'the gross inadequacy of [their] funding... makes a mockery of these good intentions'.

Producers Versus Consumers?

It can now be seen that while awareness of the needs of the consumer within the public sector has advanced over the past few years, there are still major barriers to genuine consumer choice and representation; this is ascribed by many commentators to a continuing practice amongst public sector organisations and employees of placing the interests and perspectives of the service provider over and above those of the consumer; it has been labelled 'Producerism' by Martin Smith, who defines it as 'the habit of producing things without sufficient regard to the requirements of the consumer'. Along similar lines, the Labour Party's Labour Co-Ordinating Committee asked in a 1984 publication, 'Go Local To Survive': 'How are you going to get workers to drop their traditional assumption that the client or consumer is an irritant that gets in the way of work rather than the reason for work itself?'

Changing The Corporate Culture

One solution to 'producerism', defined by Clarke and Stewart in their book, 'Getting Closer To The Public', is to change the perspective from 'services to the public' to 'services for the public', an approach supported by Gloucestershire County Council, which says that the council needs to 'break down the barrier of thinking it knows what's good for the community, and instead ask the community itself'.

This attitude may extend beyond the actual 'producers' of services (workers directly employed in refuse collection, housing repair, etc) to managers and professionals. As 'Getting Closer To The Public' further comments: 'Councillors and officers may truly believe that they know what the public wants and needs; but, in fact, these beliefs are often assumptions based on limited evidence'.

The Local Government Training Board believes that changing this approach may not have anything to do with increasing resources to the public sector.

It quotes one councillor as saying; 'Many of these things we're talking about in fact will not cost money. It's just attitude, that's what we're talking about. Improving the image with the attitude towards the public. And I believe that in many instances, although local government serves the public, elements of it appear to resent serving the public'.

All the local authorities and health authorities we visited during the course of our research, along with some other public sector organisations such as the Post Office, recognised the importance of securing this change in attitude among their staff. This was seen by most in terms of a fundamental change in the corporate culture of their organisation towards awareness of and provision for the customer - a task achieved through promotion of the 'core values' and mission statements we discuss in Chapter 3. This process was explicitly seen as going well beyond any superficial 'charm school' for employees or attempts to appeal to the customer through cosmetic changes, such as repainting vehicles.

Employee Involvement And Commitment From The Top

Most organisations estimated that they had been reasonably successful in achieving a positive employee response to the changed culture, as shown in the many suggestions made by employees during customer-orientated 'Service Days', etc. By definition, cultural change within the organisation cannot be achieved without a change of attitudes amongst its employees, and this places the question of employee involvement, and hence personnel management, firmly at the centre of any customer care strategy within the public sector; this, however, can be a difficult issue. As Deming suggests, employee involvement can be a 'cop-out' unless employees are genuinely involved in the running of their organisations.

Many local authorities have taken the need for employee involvement to mean a policy of staff care or support. Birmingham City Council, for example, has instigated an extensive staff programme on dealing with aggression which recognises that vulnerable 'front-line' employees, who have to deal with potentially difficult clients, are more likely to adopt the council's consumer approach if they can feel the council is looking after them too. Along similar lines, Wrekin District Council has always promoted its customer care policy on the basis of its efforts to become and to remain a model employer.

Like customer care generally, this concern and support for staff essentially requires commitment from top management; this includes giving staff the freedom and responsibility to act on their own initiative in dealing with the customer - an increasingly important factor in customer care. As Clarke and Stewart say 'If staff respond effectively to members of the public, they must have adequate scope in which to act; and they must also have a clear idea of what they can and cannot do on their own initiative. This means they should have all the necessary managerial and political support' ('Getting Closer To The Public', 1986).

INVOLVING THE WORKFORCE

But, as Deming suggests, involving employees more closely in customer care, while essential, is not necessarily without its problems. Some of these were apparent in the health authorities and other organisations which had introduced various forms of staff involvement. Ranging from Trent Health Authority's 'Caring For The Carers' and Peterborough Health Authority's 'Employee Charter', to the promotion of participative team briefings in the Post Office, these have received a mixed response from employees. The Union of Communications Workers, for example, has a national policy of non-cooperation with team briefings, which was reflected in our local study. The major problem has been that while the staff-centred proposals have set out to improve conditions for staff as part of promoting an improved consumer perspective, they have been unable to deal with the more fundamental problems of low pay and staff shortages.

This is, of course, in many ways an irreconcilable issue for public sector organisations faced with severe financing problems. Some local authorities, however, have shown that it is possible to combine the drive for employee commitment to customer care with an appropriate financial reward, the most obvious example of which is performance-related pay; this is provided to managers in most of the organisations covered in the book, although not necessarily based on defined quality of customer care objectives. Less commonly, team based systems of bonus payment, or profit-sharing schemes, can be used to motivate employees within 'direct' services to work around a customer care orientation. The major examples of such systems within our study were those at Braintree District Council, which had introduced an incremental pay scale for its manual workforce based on performance appraisal with a quality component, and Gloucestershire County Council and Teignbridge District Council. The latter two authorities had introduced, respectively, a team-based bonus scheme based on achieving improvements in customer care and a profit-sharing scheme which gave manual employees a clear incentive to achieve consumer satisfaction (see Chapter 4).

Trade Unions, Pay And Conditions

In general, the public sector's moves towards customer care have not been accompanied by industrial conflict. In some areas, however, such as Camden, trade union opposition has sometimes been a factor preventing the council from putting some of its ideas into operation, such as direct communications with the workforce. As Edmund Heery points out in 'Decentralisation and Democracy' (School for Advanced Urban Studies, edited by Paul Hoggett and Robin Hambleton), ironically, it is often authorities in the left-led, Labour controlled and inner-city councils which have the most opposition from unions in putting customer care ideas, such as decentralisation, into effect.

Heery advances three possible explanations for this paradox. One is that, for a complex set of political and historical reasons, trade union organisation tends to be stronger in the traditional Labour strongholds. Secondly, Labour councils have tended to be relatively generous employers and thus have perhaps raised expectations which subsequent cuts in resources have left them unable to satisfy. And thirdly, as Heery puts it, 'left Labour councils have proved determined innovators' in ways that not always appealed to the traditional perspectives of the trade unions. A central example given by Heery is the determination by the GLC to restructure its grading system along 'equal opportunities' lines. While the initiative was generally welcomed by NALGO, the minority white-collar union at the GLC, it encountered opposition both by manual groups at the workplace and also, more extensively, by the majority white-collar union, the GLC Staff Association (then organising 17,000 APT&C employees in contrast to NALGO's 3,000). The GLCSA eventually took industrial action against the proposals because, while it was prepared to see some erosion of barriers between the grades, it refused to accept a single authority-wide structure for the whole of the white-collar workforce.

Who Are 'Us And Them?'

In general, the trade unions have adapted to the innovatory policies adopted by many public sector organisations. The local authority manual workers'job evaluation structure was, for example, overhauled in 1987, with the agreement of both sides, to give 'caring' jobs, which have been done traditionally by females, a much higher rating.

More fundamentally, however, trade unions have often seen total quality management as a challenge to the central rationale of trade unionism as a collective group-based activity. This fundamental difference of approach was summed up in a 'Financial Times' report on a TGWU strike in 1989 at British Airways, a well-known pioneer of customer care policies:

> 'The strike... was called in support of an air stewardess who was dismissed for irregular drinks sales.. But the strike represents much more than that. It is a clash between the new British Airways corporate culture of human-resource management and customer service, and the TGWU's traditional culture of collective solidarity'

(Jimmy Burns, Financial Times, 19 August 1989).

The trade union information service, the Labour Research Department, has commented critically on the total quality management approach. An article in its August 1989 issue of 'Labour Research' says 'that 'there is concern in the trade union movement that, in bypassing existing channels of trade union organisation, managers are attempting to remould relationships at work - to the advantage of the employer'. Examples of this alleged strategy are listed, including team briefings, quality circles, performance-related pay and the break-up of national bargaining.

Or Just Plain Old-Fashioned Conservatism?

We have shown that some of the fundamental bargaining issues, such as low pay within the NHS and local authorities, prove a barrier to employee acceptance of a 'corporate culture'. Finally, however, a major obstacle to promoting consumer orientation within the public sector can be identified as the familiar personnel problem, 'resistance to change'.

Clark and Stewart identify twelve common objections by local authority staff and councillors to 'getting closer' to the public. These include:

- Fear of criticism from the public

- Fear of losing control over junior staff

- Uncertainty over future implications

- Lack of time

- 'I can't do it, I don't know how'.

- 'We already know what they think'.

- 'It'll undermine the democratic process'.

The manager involved in introducing a customer car policy into Blythe Valley Council similarly identifies both 'spoken' and 'unspoken' objections:

Spoken Objections

- They could not afford the time.

- They could not do training during the week.

- They would prefer not to do training at weekends.

Unspoken Objections

- Fear of what was going to happen.

- Fear about what was going to be said about them.

- Worry about what they might say about others.

Like most objections to the new and unknown, these can be, and have been overcome, through the kind of combination of communications and training now being used by a large number of public sector organisations in order to achieve change. Nevertheless, the task should not be underestimated. A vital component of any customer care strategy must be the motivation of the workforce. This means that personnel management has a central role to play. In the following chapters we look at how a variety of organisations have coped.

Chapter 2

WHO ARE THE CUSTOMERS AND WHAT DO THEY WANT?

Quality Guideline 1: Quality Begins With Delighting The Customers

'Customers must get what they want, when they want it and how they want it. An organisation must strive not only to satisfy the customers' expectations. This is the least one should do. A company should also strive to delight customers, giving them even more than they imagined possible. Your bosses may be ecstatic, the Board of Directors blissful, and your company may be considered a legend on Wall Street. But if your customers are not delighted, you have not begun to achieve quality.' **(From 'A Practical Approach To Quality', Joiner Associates Of Madison, Wisconsin.)**

Before an organisation can start to improve its customer care it must know who its customers are and what they want or need. In some cases, especially in the public sector, clients may be involuntary 'customers' (eg patients in the NHS or children taken into care). Many have no idea of what services should or could provide for them. The view of the 'father' of 'total quality' management techniques, W. Edwards Deming, is that even in the private sector the customer 'does not know what he or she will need in one, two, three, five years from now'. This means that organisations must stay ahead in deciding what the customer will want in the future. How can these aims be achieved?

In this chapter we look at:

* Who Is The Customer?

* Finding Out What The Customer Wants

* Involving The Customer

WHO IS THE CUSTOMER?

A basic distinction exists between the sale of private sector goods and services and the provision of public services; in the latter (Civil Service, NHS, local government and education), there is generally a separation of payment for services from their use. Most public services are provided free at the point of delivery (or are heavily subsidised) and are paid for out of public funds.

The immediate consequence of this division is that, in general, the 'customers' are not limited in their choice by the amount of money they have to spend; the choices the individual makes when purchasing goods or services from the private sector are therefore removed, and are replaced by a broader community interest in how much public services cost and levels of service that are provided.

This means that the user of public services cannot simply be considered as a 'customer'. The public service 'customer' has a more limited right of choice, which is exercised through the political process, rather than in the market place.

For example, individual householders cannot choose how their refuse is collected, be it by the local council's workforce or by a private contractor - this decision is taken for the community by the local council within the confines of the law. But an individual householder has some degree of influence through the ballot box on how this service is provided.

Because of this, a number of terms are used by public sector organisations to indicate their recognition of, and respect for, the needs of service users as consumers. This wide range of definitions includes: 'customers', 'consumers' 'users', 'clients', 'citizens', 'patients', and 'the public'.

Among these definitions, the word of 'citizen' has been selected in some cases to represent the service user as a responsible, active individual concerned to make a contribution to and take part in deciding the content of public services.

Uncooperative Service Users

However, this definition of the public service user as 'citizen' appears to be something of an idealisation of the real 'customers' often dealt with by local authority staff, some of whom may be violent. There is also the case of a child taken into care, in which the parent, let alone the child, may not wish to be a 'consumer' of public services. There are other instances of uncooperative public service users, such as local authority tenants in arrears with their rent; this was raised by Birmingham City Council staff on a customer care course, who asked whether the priority when collecting rent arrears should be helping the 'customer' or meeting the council's needs. The council suggested that staff should use a customer care approach to find out why the tenant was unable to pay, rather than seeing the task of collecting the rent as all-important. Ironically, Arun District Council staff have raised the question of whether the process of extracting a fee from people using the council car parking facilities can be looked on as an example of customer care!

The Vulnerable Client

Other 'unwilling' service users are the vulnerable groups, such as the elderly, the physically and mentally ill, people with disabilities, children in care, etc, who may not be able to make choices about the way they are treated. The

National Council for Voluntary Organisations, in its report 'Clients' Rights' (NCVO 1984), emphasises the need to give clients some dignity in what are often oppressive and humiliating circumstances. Along similar lines, the work of the King's Fund Centre on priority care groups in the NHS starts by emphasising the value, needs and rights of the individual receiving primary health care.

Internal and External Customers

A very different issue, raised by the application of private sector quality improvement measures within the public sector, is the concept of the 'internal customer'. In many private companies, such as the Ford Motor Company or Avon Cosmetics, the worker on the production line is regarded as equally responsible for quality service as the dealer or sales representative. Similarly, within local government, there is a growing idea that support departments, such as finance or personnel, must play a major role in meeting the needs of their 'customers' in departments like housing or recreation: Braintree District Council, which has established all its departments as independent, competing cost centres, is a good example. Within local government in particular, this change may be a direct result of the client/contractor split required by compulsory competitive tendering legislation.

FINDING OUT WHAT THE CUSTOMER WANTS

Once the 'customer' has been identified, organisations must then find out what these customers want.

Any sophisticated method of improving and maintaining quality is irrelevant unless it is based on some kind of assessment of the requirements of the service user. Public sector organisations have become increasingly conscious of this. Their efforts to ascertain the views and requirements of their consumers can be divided into two main groups: conventional methods such as consumer surveys and opinion polls, and more radical approaches exemplified by decentralisation, opening up services and 'direct democracy' based on the participation of user groups.

Customer Surveys

Customer surveys have been used by almost all the organisations in this publication. Some, such as Wrekin District Council, see these surveys as central to their entire customer orientation. In a publication entitled 'In Research of Customers (a reference to Peters and Waterman's 'In Search of Excellence'), the council presents the results of several major and a number of minor research exercises which have been undertaken to identify and monitor customer views and preferences.

Other organisations which have focused on this method of consumer response are Gloucestershire County Council, Peterborough and Trent Health Authorities, the Northern Ireland Department of Economic Development, and British Airways. Stroud College of Further Education has instituted a more systematic, computerised system of monitoring customer attitudes through SPOC/EPOC (Student Perception of Colleges and Employer Perception of Colleges) questionnaires. These are available to organisations throughout the further and higher education system.

The authors of 'The Wrekin Approach' (Local Government Studies, Jan/Feb 1989) make the point that the information obtained by these surveys can be used at several levels. At the first level, policy development, the council obtained views about decentralisation which have now been incorporated into the design of its first 'Local Shop'. At the operational level, the survey revealed a considerable degree of dissatisfaction with housing repairs and maintenance, which has now led to a substantial revision of these services.

Identification of these levels highlights the distinction the authors also make between the survey goal of measuring satisfaction between services and that of consumer response within particular services. Along these lines, the overall residents' attitude survey has triggered several smaller user surveys relating to individual services.

The results of these surveys do not always make comfortable reading for the organisations concerned, sometimes for unexpected reasons. For example, a major finding in both Wrekin and Gloucestershire councils' surveys was the degree of public ignorance of services. A similar finding was obtained from a survey carried out by Strathclyde Regional Council, which showed that only 23 per cent of residents knew that the council provided schools and education and only 26 per cent knew it provided roads.

This ignorance appears to predominate over satisfaction or dissatisfaction with the services themselves, so that the general picture was of a population happy enough with the services they were receiving, but lacking in knowledge of their content and origin.

Opinion Polls

Another way of monitoring customer satisfaction with public services is through opinion polls. These have normally shown higher than expected levels of appreciation. A recent 'Which?' poll, for example, showed considerable satisfaction with local government services among the public. The survey, published in the March 1989 issue of 'Which?' magazine showed that 78 per cent of people think that, overall, local authority services are good value for money. It also found that most people who have used local authority services are satisfied with them.

Similarly, in the NHS, the fifth in a series of annual polls carried out by the National Association of Health Authorities (NAHA) and the Society of Family Practitioner Committees indicated high levels of satisfaction, with 72 per cent describing the services as extremely, very or fairly good, although this varied between social classes.

Some of the most extensive polls for local authorities have been carried out by the Market and Opinion Research Institute (MORI) which polls residents in each area requested and summarises and compares the results. Braintree District Council is an example of one local authority which has done particularly well in such an opinion poll, coming 'top' of all district councils with over 71 per cent of its residents satisfied with the way the council is run. The survey also showed that staff at Braintree came top of the list, with 83 per cent of residents approving of their friendly and helpful attitude, while refuse collectors outshone even this result with 93 per cent of the residents pleased with the service.

MORI polls and other 'objective' methods of assessment of consumer satisfaction are clearly valuable in helping a public sector organisation to know where it stands with its users. However, Jenny Potter, in 'Consumerism and the Public Sector' (in Public Administration,1988), points out some of the dangers:

'The motto seems to be: if in doubt, carry out a survey. The particular advantage of surveys is that they seek the views of a representative sample of people, rather than simply of those who are determined enough to volunteer their opinions. But many questions can never be fully explored through structured questionnaires. And sometimes surveys are carried out without the necessary skills, and without a commitment to act on the results'.

Surveys are also an expensive business. Braintree's commissioning of MORI, for example, cost £36,000. Gloucestershire County Council used a local educational institution. Bristol Business School, to carry out its survey. It was unsure whether it could afford the use of a professional body like MORI.

INVOLVING THE CUSTOMER

A more direct and, some would argue more effective method of ascertaining consumer opinion is to involve the users of a service directly in the development of service provision. This approach includes three main dimensions:

* Greater accessibility to and information about public services

* Decentralisation of services

* 'Direct democracy', or representation of users on council committees, etc.

Getting Closer To The Public

A number of initiatives have been taken to improve relations with the public, ranging from Chief Executives making themselves available in reception areas to public service managers holding 'meet the public' sessions. The Chief Executive of Braintree District Council, for example, has made a point of regularly spending time in the reception area of the council offices so that he can gain a representative idea of consumer complaints and concerns; the same manager also goes out with refuse collection and other technical service crews when he can. The LGTB recommends this as good practice, suggesting that local authorities should 'give senior management time to walk their locality, visiting and listening to customers' ('Getting Closer To The Public', LGTB).

Along similar lines, at Royal Mail Letters in Glasgow all Consumer Care Unit staff were sent on street delivery rounds early in the customer training programme, while at London Underground a number of line managers have made themselves available to meet passengers for coffee mornings and 'drop-in' sessions (for example, on the Northern Line). Predictably, this has increased the number of complaints, but it is also clear that passengers appreciate having the opportunity to meet management and discuss the service. One of the objections to 'getting closer to the customer' identified among local government staff by Clarke and Stewart is the fear that 'The public will be critical'. But one lesson drawn from the experience of Wrekin District Council is that 'the organisation must be prepared to take some risks and ask its customers, in a structured and coherent way, what they think of the council's policies and its delivery of services'.

Opening Up The Town Halls

More radical ways of obtaining what Clarke and Stewart refer to as 'two-way communication' are identified in a booklet issued by the National Union of Public Employees (NUPE) entitled 'Better Services'. NUPE focuses on the three steps identified by the National Consumer Council for assessing the quality of services:

- identifying needs

- setting objectives

- measuring achievements.

NUPE makes a number of suggestions on how to identify consumers' needs. It sets out consumers' legal rights to council information, contained in the 1985 Local Government (Access to Information) Act. Going beyond this, the booklet shows how authorities like Leeds City Council have made an extra effort to provide information to and obtain views from its public, opening up all council meetings and also trying to include external bodies, such as local health authorities, on its joint committees. Another example is Derbyshire County Council, which launched a campaign for its consumers based on the slogan 'We're here to help you'. This was promoted in posters on buses, TV, radio and cinema advertising, on billboards and through the local paper. As a result many people realised for the first time that they were eligible for benefits and other kinds of help.

Joint Customer/Employee Committees

NUPE has also drawn up, along with Services to Community Action And Trade Unions (SCAT), a strategy for improving social services through joint consumer-employee committees. As a further example of such involvement, the NUPE booklet describes the community enquiry set up by Sheffield City Council to establish the views of local groups and feed them back into the council. This enquiry was carried out by a steering group of representatives from voluntary, statutory and non-statutory groups, together with one councillor and one council officer, and received 120 submissions from over 300 groups.

Decentralising Service Provision

One of the most radical ways in which service user involvement can be improved is through decentralisation, a strategy now being adopted by an increasing number of councils and health authorities. In the case of local authorities, this normally involves some form of physical relocation of services away from the central offices, through the establishment of 'Neighbourhood Offices'. One example is the London Borough of Islington, which has established 24 neighbourhood offices. Area committees are another way in which the effectiveness of representative democracy can be improved by bringing together residents from the same area to discuss issues relating to their ward. This establishes a level of decision-making below local authority level and can be extended, as in Walsall and Tower Hamlets, to give such committees decision-making powers. In SLD controlled Tower Hamlets, in fact, the council has effectively replaced its service committees with a system of seven area committees (mini town halls), exercising direct power within the locality.

'Direct Democracy'

The purpose of this form of decentralisation is to bring services closer to the consumer, but sometimes this has to be taken further in order to provide the service users with a genuine opportunity for involvement in the way they are run. As one writer says (Hambleton, 'Consumerism, Decentralisation and Democracy', 'Public Administration', 1988), 'it is clear that in several local authorities decentralisation strategies are having an impact which goes beyond 'surface only' change'. The London Borough of Islington, for example, has supplemented its Neighbourhood Offices with a system of Neighbourhood Forums in which public and community groups from the area are represented, with positive action in the form of guaranteed places for disadvantaged groups. Each forum is given a budget, which in 1988 was around £60,000 each.

Perhaps the most radical involvement of direct users was pioneered by the Greater London Council (GLC) with its project to decentralise influence and power to groups rather than areas. While the representation of women, ethnic minorities and other groups with specific interests on GLC committees ended with the authority's abolition, the concept has survived in some other

Labour-controlled councils with 'user groups' having a direct say in the running of, for example, such services as leisure and recreation, transport and childcare. Perhaps the oldest example of a 'user group' is the traditional tenants' association, many of which still flourish on council housing estates.

But these examples of active consumer involvement are rare in the public sector; Jenny Potter argues that, 'Consumerism alone is not enough to overcome public apathy' (Consumerism And The Public Sector, RIPA 1988). The attitude survey carried out by Gloucestershire County Council, which found that consumers were largely unaware of which services were provided by the council, shows that it is ignorance rather than active hostility that is the main enemy of public service organisations.

But this can be overcome; as the examples on user involvement show, there are many strategies open to organisations to win public support. The publicising of council meetings may in itself by effective, as Harlow Council discovered when it issued a series of eye-catching posters publicising the meetings; this resulted in much larger public attendances.

Chapter 3
MEETING CUSTOMER NEEDS

'Our company mission is to provide what our customers require, though all means available to us, so that both our company and our Capital City continue to prosper'. **(London Underground's Mission Statement)**

Once an organisation has found out, by the various means available, who its customers are and what its customers want, it must then decide how to meet these requirements. In this chapter we look at the various methods adopted to improve customer care. These include:

- Developing A Corporate Identity

- Reorganisation

- Performance Indicators/Standards

- Complaints Procedures

- Quality Improvement Projects

- Decentralisation

- Accessibility For The Customer ·

However, we first look at the question of how many of the various private sector management theories and techniques are appropriate to the public sector.

PRIVATE AND PUBLIC - BREAKING DOWN BARRIERS?

While the original ideas of 'total quality' and of putting the customer first were developed within the private sector, they have now been taken up enthusiastically by many public sector organisations. But in the course of doing so the differences as well as the similarities between the two sectors have been highlighted. How much can be successfully transferred from one sector to the other?

Measuring Quality

Perhaps the biggest asset of private industry, particularly in production, is the ability to measure quality standards and outcomes in more precise ways than are easily available to public sector services. The clearest example of this is the method known as 'statistical process control', originally invented by W Edwards Deming, as a method of achieving the continuous improvement necessary for total quality within an organisation.

Statistical process control (SPC) is based on the observation of the variation in processes. For example, the owner of a car gets to know its normal sounds - its 'common cause of variation'; if these change, the driver knows immediately that something is wrong. In the same way, any repetitive process within an organisation, from machining parts to coding tax returns, can be monitored to show the variation that is a regular feature of the system (due to common causes). An important part of the quality improvement process is for the individual employee to be able to recognise special cause variation and put it right before it gets out of hand. SPC is used to establish 'control limits', based on standard measurements of processes, which enable the employee to identify quickly whether a result is due to common cause or special cause variations.

It is also possible in principle to transfer this statistical process control to administrative services within the public sector, particularly those that are the most repetitive and routine. For example, the quality of information coming into an administrative system can be equated with the quality of incoming materials in production as a factor in variation. In practice, however, few if any public sector organisations have yet begun to use such precisely statistical methods for measuring quality.

Right First Time

A more successful transfer from industrial 'total quality' methods to the area of public services has been that of 'Right First Time'. This is a Japanese management approach along the same lines as their 'Just In Time' (JIT) stock control method, now widely practised in other countries. As its name suggests, the technique ensures that employees concentrate on the quality of production rather than on output with its associated assumption that if the commodity is faulty it will be returned as a reject. One major service organisation featured in this publication which has integrated this approach into its work processes is British Telecom. BT claims: 'We are committed to far-reaching changes in our culture through Total Quality Management to enable us to meet customers' requirements first time, everytime, as part of our normal business activity'.

In practice, this commitment is expressed through a major programme of customer care training and project development which, while it may appear to take up time allocated to immediate service production, is aimed at moving the organisation away from 'fire-fighting' towards processes that work the first time round.

Within the public sector, Arun District Council has similarly concentrated on a 'right first time' approach. In its staff booklet, 'In The Customer's Shoes', the council points out that the first impression a user receives of council services is irreplaceable. In response to the objection raised by many council employees that they lack the time to deal at length with the public, the reply is that contact and consideration at this point is likely to save considerable time and energy which otherwise may be necessary at a later stage to deal with customer complaints.

Fitness and Conformance

In 'Quality and Competition', the fourth in its series on 'Competition and Local Authorities', the Local Government Training Board (LGTB) lays down guidelines on the meaning of quality; these include the distinction between the two dimensions of 'fitness' and 'conformance' which is widely used in the private sector. A common example, used by the LGTB, is that the standards used to define high quality in an Austin Metro are entirely separate from those used for a Rolls-Royce.

This relates to the 'fitness' dimension of quality, which defines the extent to which a service does what it is intended to do. 'Conformance' on the other hand, deals with the extent to which a service conforms to the specifications laid down. This has again been widely used in the private sector, for example at Avon Cosmetics, where a 'Principle Of Non-Conformance' (PONC) measurement is used by production-line employees to reduce the number of rejects.

In the public sector, the LGTB suggests that the conformance criterion can most appropriately be introduced when drawing up specifications for the services of local authorities, an increasingly important activity for them and for other organisations faced with compulsory competitive tendering. A specification, the LGTB argues, is a service design, and should be seen as an integral part of the quality management system: 'We should specify in such a way that a high quality service is likely to be delivered'.

Regarding the 'fitness' criterion, the LGTB reiterates the National Consumer Council's questions

- 'What is the service supposed to do?'

- 'What does the service actually do?'

These questions, the LGTB points out, are particularly relevant to the changing needs and interests of the public. It is all too easy to assume that a public sector organisation 'knows best what's good for its customers'.

However, as suggested in Chapter 1, this attitude is increasingly being challenged within local authorities. Arun District Council, for example, has incorporated a 'fitness' criterion into its budgeting system by asking different departments to identify their services as being either essential or desirable. The aim is do away with continuing to provide services for their own sake, and to find out whether there are new consumer interests for which the council should now be providing services.

Quality Standards and Quality Assurance

The important quality standard used within private industry - British Standard 5750 - is being sought increasingly by organisations in the public sector. The British Standards Institute (BSI), the independent organisation which issues the famous 'Kitemark', guaranteeing that products conform to national or international standards, is currently linked with a drive by the Department of Trade and Industry to promote quality in British industry.

Comparing private industry products with public sector services is problematic when it comes to applying precise quality standards, and the LGTB warns in its 'Quality and Competition' booklet that 'there is a danger that the straightforward application of British Standard 5750 will lead to an insensitive emphasis on a quality bureaucracy and a proliferation of paper'.

Nevertheless, many of the local authorities we contacted mentioned that they were considering applying for British Standard 5750 registration, although none had actually done so. The LGTB document comments: 'it will, over time, be possible to get local authority DLOs' quality assurance systems certified, but so far no authority has done this'.

Of the other organisations studied, MBS - a private computer servicing firm - is heavily involved in the process of obtaining British Standard 5750 certification and has already achieved this within its workshops. British Telecom has also registered for the standard. A major example of a service industry using one of the BSI 'special systems' is BT's 'Call Routing Apparatus Maintenance' (CRAM), which provides protection for the national telephone network by ensuring that equipment connected to the network is properly maintained.

British Standard 5750 itself sets out the national quality standards which comply with the international quality standard 1509000. The first requirement is that the organisation applying must already operate a quality system; it is asked to send its quality manual to BSI for checking. There are probably few public sector organisations currently able to meet the initial requirement of the BSI. Nevertheless, the concept of a tangible quality standard remains a valuable point of reference for public sector organisations. The LGTB sums up the position: 'Quality management in a service organisation cannot be the same as in a manufacturing organisation but the differences between services and manufactured goods do not mean that quality concepts outlined in British Standard 5750 cannot be used. However, considerable adaptation is necessary, especially if quality management is to be extended to the more subtle and complex services provided by local authorities'.

An idea that is more accessible to public sector organisations is that of 'quality assurance'. Many health authorities responded to the 1983 Griffiths Report on the NHS by instigating quality assurance programmes led by specially-appointed managers (Hambleton, 'Consumerism, Decentralisation and Local Democracy', Public Administration, 1988). Our case studies of Peterborough and Pembrokeshire health authorities and Belfast City Hospital provide examples.

In an article on 'Quality Assurance: The Professional's Role' in 'Public Money and Management' (Summer 1988), Roger Ellis considers how this system, that originated in manufacturing as a means of ensuring that products consistently satisfied customers, can be used in health care and other 'caring' professions in the public sector. He argues that three stages are required to establish a quality assurance programme:

- Identification of the aspects of the service that should be tackled

- Assessment of key variables (inputs, processes, outputs and outcomes)

- The steps taken to generate improvement through diminishing or eliminating shortfalls in service.

The author concludes that the prerequisite for success is to train professionals to identify precise specifications of both the 'product' - a caring service - and the means of its production.

The LGTB booklet on 'Quality and Competition' for local authorities also discusses quality assurance, defining it as one of the two components of quality management (the other is quality control). Quality assurance is defined as 'an attempt to develop a 'total quality' or a zero defects approach'). Clearly this, like many other quality criteria applicable to the private sector, is more difficult to achieve within the public services, and in fact many quality assurance programmes within the health service may be seen more in terms of setting high-quality standards than of achieving 'total quality'. This accommodation to reality was symbolised in the title of the programme that grew out of Pembrokeshire's Health Authority's quality assurance project, 'Aspiring To Excellence'.

Even within a relatively general framework for establishing quality assurance criteria, it is difficult for the public services to satisfactorily emulate the private sector. The LGTB suggests, instead, the use of 'quality control', which is concerned with checking the service after 'production' in order to eliminate those parts that do not reach the specified standard. This, too, is a common private sector technique but, says the LGTB, it is 'necessary and valuable and cannot be abandoned for some, perhaps unobtainable, system of assurance'. It suggests the use of quality control to check whether adequate work has been produced within direct services, either by contractors or by DLOs.

Specifications and Audits

Other areas of private sector practice now beginning to be appropriated by the public sector are, 'specifications' and 'audits', both of which are becoming increasingly necessary, particularly for local authorities and the NHS, in the era of compulsory competitive tendering. Both, however, have been used by the public sector in a somewhat different form from the primarily financially-based methods used in private industry.

The need to draw up service specifications as part of the process of tendering for direct services for example, has been used by many Labour-controlled authorities as a way of introducing community-based criteria for service quality. Camden Council, for example, uses its process of service specification to identify 'core' services essential for the well-being of the community.

The use of audits, another primarily accountancy-based method used within the private sector and promoted as a 'value for money' tool by the Audit Commission, has also been taken up by local authorities in a more quality-oriented direction. Arun District Council is about to introduce a departmental auditing system whereby managers can check that their services are conforming to a range of quality-based criteria. The Labour Party has recently proposed local quality audits for council services and the health service.

DEVELOPING A CORPORATE IDENTITY

Many organisations have sought to promote customer care by developing a strong corporate identity. This approach is useful in two ways. Firstly, possessing a corporate identity focuses employees' attention on the aims of the organisation, which in this case is developing the idea of caring about the customer. Secondly, a powerful corporate identity is a means to signpost the services an organisation provides.

One way in which many organisations have set about creating a strong sense of corporate identity among employees has been the formulation of a 'mission statement' or a set of 'core values'. However, these methods are really only useful if they constitute the starting point for a much bigger strategy. Sir Roy Griffiths, architect of many of the changes in NHS management during the 1980s warns: 'Ever since 'In Search of Excellence' all top management talk the same gobbledy gook with mission statements, etc. I am not objecting to mission statements but I am only prepared to support them providing they are followed up by detailed spelling out in precise terms so that there is some form of measurement as to how well the generalised objectives are being attained' (speaking at the Institute of Health Services Management conference, 1989).

British Telecom's 'core values', for example, have the specific aim of communicating to employees the idea that quality should be their own priority. The core values are not intended to be just 'a set of pious statements' but instead a part of a working programme designed to bring about results. A 'mission statement', linked to the core values, has also been issued and communicated to all managers.

N. Ireland Department Of Economic Development

A survey commissioned by the Northern Ireland Department of Economic Development revealed that while many of its services were popular, the public did not necessarily associate them with the department. The biggest obstacle to improving the quality of its services was the lack of central direction and clarity caused by the disparate nature of its operations. In order to solve these problems and give the organisation direction, it produced a document called 'The Aims of the Department'. These included an 'economic development aim' to strengthen the Northern Ireland Economy, an 'economic service aim' to provide the services essential to the province's economic development, and the 'management aim' to achieve efficiency and move resources into activities which would strengthen the economy. The department believes that these aims can only be achieved if the staff are committed to achieving the 'highest standards of performance in all operations and dealings with their customers'.

N. Ireland Electricity

Northern Ireland Electricity published its own core values in 1988 in a booklet entitled 'Our Corporate Aim and Objectives'. This booklet, which was distributed to all staff, states that the aim of the organisation is to 'provide our customers with electricity and service based on quality and value by always working in a responsive and effective manner'. There are also five supporting corporate objectives and values:

- 'Dedication to excellent customer service is the shared objective of everyone'.

- 'Marketing for growth, getting the best from our resources and assets, and making good investment decisions is how we manage our business'.

- 'Our organisation encourages innovation, effective decision making and responsive action'.

- 'The welfare, development and reward of staff in our organisation recognises the needs and aspirations of individuals and the commitment and contribution needed to achieve our objectives'.

- 'Our organisation is responsible and caring, it identifies with the needs of the community and is sensitive to the impact of its actions on individuals and the environment'.

The effects of this leaflet on employee commitment to customer care, however, have not necessarily been positive. It was written by management without any union consultation and this has made the unions highly suspicious that the booklet is closely linked to impending privatisation. They also believe that management behaviour is inconsistent with the sentiments expressed in 'Our Corporate Aim And Objective'.

British Airways

British Airways has attempted to improve its standards of customer care by developing a corporate culture across the whole company. It has changed its logo, uniforms and aircraft design in order to promote an identity, and it believes that this has been widely accepted by the workforce. The company's values are spelt out in the Chief Executive's 'mission statement', which is printed on a small plastic card issued to all employees. The corporate culture is also put across through promotional activities within the company.

Local Government And Education

The mission statement at Stroud College of Further Education states that the college aims to 'serve the whole community'. It backs up this overall aim by defining 'high-quality services' in terms of its ability to respond to the needs of the community in the curriculum it offers. Assessment of customer demand at the college is increasingly market-led and the college has demonstrated this priority by creating the new post of Director of Marketing.

Birmingham City Council has also sought to develop a corporate style by introducing uniforms for its manual workers. They have also been issued with calling cards to provide a professional 'image' to the public.

Arun District Council, however, does not attach much importance to developing a corporate visual identity. It believes that some organisations 'start with the logo' instead of using a new visual identity to sum up the progress made towards providing a good quality of service to the public. The council is considering developing core values but only if they actually help to develop positive employee attitudes to customer care.

REORGANISATION

The development of a customer care strategy is often achieved through the re-organisation of departments or of the business as a whole. Sometimes a re-organisation is a prerequisite if service quality is to be improved.

Royal Mail Letters, Glasgow

Royal Mail Letters in Glasgow is one example. The Post Office was divided into four separate businesses (Counters, Parcels, Letters and Giro Bank) on

1 October 1986. Following on from this re-organisation, specialist Customer Care departments were set up throughout the various Post Office businesses. In Glasgow, the Royal Mail Letters 'Customer Care Unit' superseded the 'Correspondence Branch', which had previously dealt with enquiries and complaints as part of its work. With the establishment of the Customer Care Unit, the number of staff was increased from eight to 25 and these employees now work solely on customer care issues.

A 'Business Customer Care Unit' was later established in 1988 to provide a similar service for the Post Office's business customers. The importance of maintaining good links with the business community was recognised by the Post Office, especially as the Post Office's letter monopoly was then under threat. In addition to its customer care obligations, staff also have a sales role and are responsible for increasing the level of business post. A further 25 staff deal with undeliverable items of mail and handle postcode enquiries.

British Airways

British Airways has also restructured its business. Some of its regional bases (Birmingham, Manchester and Scotland) have been established as independent Strategic Business Units and these units are expected to become self-financing through improved levels of service to the public. There has also been an increasing decentralisation of departmental functions. The Human Resources function has been devolved to line management, and the Human Resources Department slimmed down to a nucleus of staff who now perform a consultancy role for line managers. The changes are aimed not only at saving money through reductions in the numbers of staff employed, but also at enabling line managers to build up a greater rapport with their staff. In turn it is hoped that this will be reflected in better levels of care for the customer.

London Underground

London Underground announced its intention of restructuring its business in its Managing Director's 'mission statement' of 1 November 1988. This restructuring is also linked explicitly to London Underground's policies to improve customer care. Management of train services will be divided into ten tube lines as opposed to the previous four divisions. Managers of these lines will be responsible to a newly appointed Passenger Services Director. Both the Passenger Services Director and the line managers will be expected to meet profit, quality and safety targets. London Underground's managing director stresses that the major theme of the re-organisation is that 'the customer is the only reason we exist'.

London Borough Of Camden

In order to provide more effective and accountable services, the London Borough of Camden is now merging its disparate departments into five corporate teams headed by Chief Officers. Recreation, libraries, planning, transport, engineering and environmental health will, for example, all be merged into a new Environmental Services Unit. The technical services will be brought together as a Direct Services Organisation (although this is facing opposition from the trade unions).

This proposed re-organisation will mean that council strategy will be determined by a management team led by the Chief Executive and consisting of Chief Officers from the five service departments. The aim of the re-organisation is to make senior management more responsible for the money spent and also more directly accountable for the services provided to the public. The council believes that if one person is ultimately responsible for the service and the customer is informed of this, then the customer will know where to complain and there will be fewer barriers placed in the way of the customer making the complaint.

PERFORMANCE INDICATORS/STANDARDS

The Government White Paper on the NHS, 'Working for Patients', puts much emphasis on the importance of improving customer care in the health service. This emphasis has recently been echoed by Duncan Nichol, the Chief Executive of the NHS Management Executive, who made 'quality management' an NHS review topic for 1989. By the autumn of 1989, all regional health authorities should have made preparations to implement quality assurance projects and criteria to judge performance.

A number of organisations, however, have already run projects designed to improve the quality of their services. These projects are often based around developing standards against which performance can be judged. Belfast City Hospital, for example, decided that its standards of performance should reflect existing performance, except where these standards could be improved by staff. It was also decided that these standards should be decided by the staff who operate the services.

'Standards Of Care'

For example, West Dorset Health Authority has produced written 'standards of care' to measure the quality of care. The authority wanted to ensure high standards of care and prove that people were receiving high quality services. The following are examples of the 'standards of care' used in West Dorset HA:

- 'Physical examinations or treatments took place in an area completely screened from view'.

- 'Clothes or gowns provided by the health authority adequately covered the body'.

- 'The patient was encouraged to participate in his/her own health care'.

- 'The patient was given the opportunity to make routine decisions (eg choice of food, bathing times, etc.)'

There are now over 300 written 'standards of care' used at West Dorset HA and these are reviewed and updated at least once every six months. Topics that have regularly arisen out of this process have been written up as 'District Standards' and these are in line with 'Wessex Regional Standards'.

Paramedical staff groups have followed the example established by nursing staff and are now producing their own standards. The authority also plans to introduce a 'Patients Charter' which will lay down the rights of people during their stay in hospital. 'Standards of care', which relate directly to the charter, are also being produced. This will enable managers to ensure that staff follow the charter. It is also planned to ask a random selection of people to complete a questionnaire on the quality of service they receive from the hospital.

'Value Statements'

As already noted, the Northern Ireland Department of Economic Development, has produced a statement of the aims of the department. In order to make this statement relevant to every-day work, the department has also produced a 'Value Statement' which stresses specific values and principles that the staff should apply to their work. Staff workshops were run to promote the 'Value Statement' and ideas have emerged from these to improve the quality of service. Staff working in the Youth Training Division, for example, decided that decentralising their division would be the most effective way of improving services.

Private Sector Examples

One private sector organisation has adopted a system by which employees are required to focus on their own contribution to the company. It asks them to define who their customers are and how they can improve services to these customers. A measuring system will help employees assess the effects of their plans and determine whether they have moved from their existing level of customer service towards their defined objectives.

Another organisation, MBS Services - the distributing and servicing section of a computer manufacturing company - has been trying to get accreditation by the British Standards Institute (BS5750) as a means of establishing standards of service quality. The Hull branch has already obtained this accreditation.

COMPLAINTS PROCEDURES

In the Post Office, Royal Mail Letters has clearly defined targets for delivering first and second class letters. It is recognised, however, that complaints from the public about the quality of service cannot be entirely eliminated, and that these should be treated effectively and promptly. It has therefore laid down maximum time limits for complaints and enquiries to be answered. These range from five days for a single missing letter, to six weeks for a serious complaint such as the loss of a registered letter. The performance of the Royal Mail in meeting these deadlines is monitored through questionnaires which are sent to customers who have made a complaint. Rewards are offered to customer care units which meet the enquiry targets and provide a good service. The Glasgow Customer Care Unit also produces a list of delivery 'failures' each month for the local delivery offices. These are used by the offices to ensure that service standards are maintained by identifying and rectifying the causes of these 'failures'.

QUALITY IMPROVEMENT PROJECTS

Many organisations believe that one way to begin improving services is to concentrate effort on projects in a single department or service area. These projects are sometimes run as part of a corporate policy that applies across the whole organisation, but they can also be organised in a single department which is then given a large measure of local autonomy.

In Belfast City Hospital, for example, quality assurance projects were set up in specific areas of the hospital. The aim behind the projects was to achieve improvements in the quality of service across the whole units or departments. A myriad number of projects has been run in the Geriatric Medical Unit covering the following six areas:

- **Personal services,** including laundry facilities and meal times;

- **Social activities,** including the provision of music, church services, story telling and afternoon teas;

- **Treatment and therapy,** which was improved with the establishment and maintenance of individual care plans for all patients;

- **The work environment,** which was improved by repainting and the introduction of aquariums, caged birds, paintings, and plants.

- **Dealing with relatives,** which was improved through the establishment of a relatives' group. (Despite initial enthusiasm, this has not been overly successful, primarily because the interest of many relatives varies after the discharge or death of their relative. The unit also plans to introduce an information leaflet for relatives with the help of local sponsorship.)

- **Staffing,** which despite some recruitment and retention difficulties, has provided a high standard of care.

Trent Regional Health Authority managers say that the most effective way of improving the quality of its service to the public is to publicise examples of good health service practice. The authority claims to have achieved this aim

35

by inviting its districts to run pilot projects and to then display the results at a conference. It hopes that all parts of the region will benefit from these examples by spreading the experience gained of good practice to other districts. Five pilot projects were run and details of these were incorporated into a booklet and video package called 'From Me To You'. The package is now widely used by management to improve the quality of services in Trent RHA.

One of the five pilot projects was carried out at the North Derbyshire Accident and Emergency Department. As a result of a patient questionnaire, and the efforts of a group of volunteer health service workers dedicated to improving the quality of care (known as the Patient Service Team), a number of changes have been made to the department. These include improved information for patients, and better facilities in the waiting rooms.

Liverpool Health Authority is planning to introduce a 'Quality Management Programme' which aims simply to 'maintain and improve the quality of our health care and service provision'. In order to achieve this aim, four requirements are identified:

- **A Quality Management Culture** which has clear direction and organisational goals. These goals should be regularly communicated so that they become the 'shared property of all managers, employers and service users'.

- **A Quality Management Structure** composed of a 'Quality Panel' at district level and 'Quality Steering Groups' at unit level. This is the co-ordination network 'through which all information relevant to the programme will be communicated'.

- **A Quality Management Model** for practical use by any unit, team or individual to measure the quality of the service it provides.

- **Quality Management Tools and Resources** that can be used to improve service quality.

These objectives recognise that effective management structures geared to improving the quality of service need to be backed up by the 'tools and resources' that are vital to running quality improvement programmes.

Projects to improve quality are also often the result of employee suggestions. These come either through the traditional staff suggestion scheme or through new types of employee consultation and working groups, such as quality circles. In Belfast City Hospital, for example, a quality circle was set up to help staff dealing with patient deaths in the hospital. As a result, a booklet containing guidelines and help for staff facing this situation was produced. Another quality circle in the gynaecology ward succeeded in persuading maintenance workers to carry out minor repairs which had previously been neglected.

At Arun District Council, staff discussions under the 'Working For The Public' programme led to over 400 suggestions being made. A number of these have already been implemented, including fitting sliding doors in the council's reception area, improving interview rooms in reception, and providing umbrellas for the open walkway between the swimming pool and sports centre.

DECENTRALISATION

Decentralisation of services can be another of improving service provision to the customer. The rationale behind this strategy is that moving the service closer to the customer will ensure more responsiveness to clients' needs. Functions which were previously carried out by central departments have often been devolved. This is particularly true of functions which are connected with 'front-line' services. At Birmingham City Council, for example, the public relations department has been devolved so that it can work effectively to promote local activities and issues. A small media section has been left at the centre.

One health authority decided to divide its services into five 'localities' and then devolved management responsibility for its community services to these. The five localities were designed to share boundaries with the 24 local council neighbourhood offices grouped in clusters of four or five. It also followed up the recommendations of the Cumberlege Report on nursing care in the community by introducing neighbourhood nursing teams. These were attached to the five localities.

According to one manager, the effects of decentralising to locality level has been mostly beneficial. She believes that the establishment of localities has:

- Improved communication between staff and management;

- Led to improved budgeting, which has released extra resources to improve services;

- Resulted in locality managers promoting their local communities;

- Improved the environment of the health centres, which are now better organised and decorated.

Gloucestershire County Council

The decentralisation of departments and services is also seen as a key strategy for improving customer care at Gloucestershire County Council. As part of this process, the managerial hierarchy has been restructured and the number of staff working in the central offices reduced by at least one third.

Area provision has been expanded, particularly in social services. In addition, the authority has introduced cost centre management or 'local resource management' - a terminology preferred because the issues considered are not just budgetary but include management of human resources, administration of buildings, and taking advantage of opportunities for income generation.

A major reason behind decentralisation is that it increases the responsibility and autonomy given to management. It is hoped that this will be directed towards the goal of customer care and that the philosophy of taking responsibility for improved services will pervade the rest of the organisation, including support as well as direct service departments.

ACCESSIBILITY FOR THE CUSTOMER

Increasing the accessibility of services to the public has been one of the more practical moves towards developing customer care. Wrekin District Council, for example, has opened a number of 'local shops' in high street locations throughout the borough to give residents more access to council services and council officers. A MORI survey of residents' interests commissioned by the council had revealed that the concentration of council services around Telford shopping centre was limiting the public's access.

Northern Ireland Electricity has recently introduced lunchtime and Saturday opening for its retail outlets as a way of improving the quality of service to the public. It has also introduced a new range of brand-name goods into the shops to increase revenue and make the extended opening hours more economically viable. Arun District Council also introduced lunchtime opening for its 'front-line services' offices in 1988. It is now examining whether the flexi-time system introduced to accompany lunchtime opening is being worked in favour of the customer as well as the employee.

Further Education Access

Stroud College of Further Education has introduced a number of schemes designed to bring it in touch with the wider community and increase the accessibility of its courses. These include a programme of Open Learning (a community-based equivalent of the Open University in adult education), and the employment of an access tutor in order to extend course provision to a greater number of adults. There is also a special tutor provided for the unemployed.

These initiatives have been prompted by a drop in the number of school leavers now entering further education. The college is now concentrating on encouraging adults to return to full- or part-time education. To further this aim, a strong emphasis is placed on catering for the needs of students with disabilities and for parents with childcare difficulties. The college provides a creche and the income generated from profit-making courses is used to provide facilities for people with disabilities. The college has already trained reception staff in how to deal with students who have hearing problems, braille boards for the blind are under consideration, and the college buildings have been converted to make them wheelchair-accessible wherever possible.

Equal Opportunities

Some organisations have taken the view that the implementation of equal opportunities policies is vital if the number of people using services is to be increased.

Liverpool Health Authority has appointed a Health and Race Development Officer and a link worker for the Chinese community. It has also established a board of around 130 voluntary interpreters and translated many of its information leaflets into ethnic minority languages. All these initiatives have been strongly influenced by the health authority's desire to extend the accessibility of its services to all the people in the district.

Birmingham City Council has integrated its equal opportunities policies into all its activities for many years and these policies are now being promoted through its customer care strategy. In common with Liverpool Health Authority, Birmingham City Council puts major emphasis on increasing access to its services. All leaflets are printed in several languages and worded to secure maximum accessibility. Arun District Council accepted that many of its leaflets were worded in bureaucratic language that often had the effect of dissuading people from reading them. As a consequence it has used the Plain English Campaign to examine the wording of all its publications.

Equal opportunities that are developed to improve the representation and prospects of ethnic minorities inside organisations can also improve service delivery to the customer. Wrekin District Council believes that 'in an organisation which provides services to the community, these services are best provided by a workforce which broadly reflects the community it services'.

Birmingham City Council has an employment target of 20 per cent for ethnic minorities and this has been achieved in some areas. Targets have been reached through advertising in the ethnic minority press and by recruiting in schools and community centres. The employment-related and service-related aspects of Birmingham's equal opportunities policies have been unified in a series of 'open days' held by council departments. Social Services, for example, held a two-day event to which members of the public were invited to look at the number of jobs available in the department and also to gain a better understanding of the way the service operates. At present, only 2.8 per cent of Liverpool Health Authority's staff are from ethnic minorities, compared to the 8.8 per cent in the population as a whole, but strong efforts are now being made to improve the representation of non-white groups in its workforce.

Chapter 4
THE PERSONNEL IMPLICATIONS

'Dr Joseph Juran, one of the other famous quality 'gurus', estimated many years ago that no more than 15% of the problems (i.e. variation) in an organisation are due to special causes (i.e. possibly, but not exclusively, the workers), leaving management with the responsibility for at least 85% of the potential improvement through changes in the system within which their employees are obliged to labour. In 1985, Dr Deming revised these figures to 6% and 94% respectively. Very often workers, if they are asked, can identify the special causes that result in difficulties and inefficiencies -after all, they are the ones that have to suffer them directly - but only management can change the actual system within which they work and which contains by far the bulk of the obstacles to improved quality, reliability and productivity'. **(The Deming Philosophy, Department of Trade Pamphlet, 1989.)**

Any systems for delivering quality services or products will not work without the vital contribution of motivated and committed workers. This makes the personnel function key to any strategy for improving services. In this chapter we look at the various ways in which organisations seek to motivate their employees to provide better services to the public. We also look at the collective bargaining implications. This chapter covers:

- Training

- Quality Circles

- Team Briefings

- Staff Suggestion Schemes

- House Magazines and Leaflets

- Employee Attitude Surveys

- Employee Appraisal Schemes

- Performance-related Pay

- Staff Support And Development

40

- Trade Union And Employee Reaction

- Changes to Employees' Pay And Conditions

TRAINING

Training is a common feature in all the customer care strategies used by the organisations in this book. Staff must be closely involved with the introduction of customer care policies into any organisation and need to identify closely with the aspirations of the organisation if customer care policies are to be successful. Therefore much of the training associated with customer care strategies concentrates on encouraging staff to make suggestions and then encouraging them to see these ideas through to fruition. Ideas raised by staff at training workshops are often followed up, for example in quality circles.

Our research found the most common type of training to be the 'workshop session', where staff are encouraged to express their own views on the services they provide. Staff awareness training, used by many organisations to introduce employees to the idea of customer care is also important.

The British Telecom approach to customer care training is typical of such training programmes and is divided into three stages:

- **Initial Awareness Training** is given to all staff and takes up a half or a whole working day. Standard packages, including videos, slide shows and discussion sessions, are presented within all districts.

- **Three-day Workshop Training** is initially targeted on senior managers, whose job it is to develop Quality Improvement Teams. Although the managers themselves are expected to 'cascade' Quality Improvement Team training down through the organisation, they are assisted by full-time trainers and facilitators.

- **Quality Improvement Team Training** in the 'tools and techniques' of customer care is given at workshops throughout the country for all 37,000 managers within the organisation, each lasting three days. As part of their training, managers are required to set up a quality improvement programme of their own. This involves setting up a team to look at problem-solving and quality improvement.

Wrekin District Council's training is made up of three separate initiatives. The first initiative takes the form of 'Service Days', when groups of staff spend a day in the training centre to examine the service they provide and to identify the barriers that prevent a high-quality service being provided to the customer. The sections then prepare action plans for improved service delivery. The second initiative consists of 'Core Days' on 'Caring for our Customers'; employees are sent initially on a day-long course of training and this training then continues within the individual's department. In Wrekin's Housing Department, for example, courses are run on the problems of homeless people. These courses include role-playing exercises.

The third initiative is a 'Communication Package', which aims to improve employees' skills in communicating with the customer. It includes training in telephone manner and letter writing.

Pembrokeshire Health Authority

The key to Pembrokeshire Health Authority's training programme, called 'Aspiring To Excellence', was a series of one-day staff events to which all employees were invited. Over 90 per cent of the staff attended the events, even though participation was voluntary. The programme itself contained audio-visual material and a series of workshop sessions on the communications, customer, human and systems 'factors' in the health authority. At the end of each event the District General Manager answered a series of questions, posed by a professional presenter, that had been raised by staff during the day.

At the workshop sessions the staff were asked to come up with ideas to improve the authority's performance. The ideas expressed at these events, together with the findings of a staff opinion survey, helped the authority to revitalise its induction programme. This led to the development of an induction course called 'Foundations', which is run over two half days for all new employees. 'Focus teams' were also established in the wake of the workshop sessions to follow up on the ideas generated by staff.

British Airways

British Airways has launched a number of training and communications initiatives as part of its customer care strategy, including a 'Day In The Life' exercise. This exercise emerged from a demand by staff for a better understanding of the way in which other departments function within the organisation. As a result, departments are encouraged to hold 'open day' demonstrations. These are run by the staff themselves (after training) at which the work of the department is presented to all employees who may be interested. Training exercises like a 'Day In The Life' are another means of informing the workforce about what the company is doing and enlisting support for its attempts to improve the quality of service.

Improving Employee Attitudes To The Public

Some local authorities concentrate more on how employees should treat the public, rather than on more general ways in which services could be improved. At Arun District Council, for example, telephone technique is taught on all training courses. It has also launched a poster campaign on the theme of 'Own That Phone', encouraging members of staff to pick up a ringing telephone and take responsibility for the enquiry, even if the call is not for that specific individual. The council believes that no member of staff should look to others to solve a problem and it is the responsibility of staff as a whole to consider the customer. At Braintree District Council employees in direct contact with the public are sent on courses on customer relations and telephone techniques.

QUALITY CIRCLES

Quality circles were first used in Japan and did not reach Britain until 1978, when Rolls-Royce introduced them. Our research found them to be most common in health authorities and in the private sector. Among the local authorities, only Arun District Council uses techniques similar to those of a quality circle - it runs 'First Impressions Groups', which are composed of staff from different parts of the authority meeting on a rotating basis. The standard quality circle model, however, is that suggested by The National Society of Quality Circles. It defines a quality circle as 'a group of four to twelve people coming from the same work area, performing similar work, who voluntarily meet on a regular basis to identify, analyse, and solve their own work-related problems'. It adds that 'the circle presents solutions to management and is usually involved in implementing and later monitoring them'.

For quality circles to succeed, the National Society of Quality Circles lists the following essential factors:

* Voluntary participation;

* The support of top management;

* Operational management support;

* The presence of a facilitator to guide the circle;

* Training for all members of the circle;

* A shared work background for participants;

* An orientation towards finding solutions, not simply a means for discussion;

* Recognition of success from management.

Health Authority Quality Circles

Liverpool Health Authority has closely followed the National Society of Quality Circles guidelines and has given its staff free rein to consider subjects, albeit with some important qualifications. These are that quality circles are not allowed to discuss conditions of service, employment policies, grievances, disputes or individual personalities.

A good example of a multi-disciplinary quality circle is the Elderly Unit Quality Circle established by Peterborough Health Authority. It consists of two nurses, one physiotherapist, a member of the catering staff, one porter, a person from medical records and a 'facilitator' from the Quality Assurance Department. The chair of the quality circle is elected by its members. Managers often take part in the quality circles at Peterborough HA but the circles are not management led. The only restraint on the quality circles is that the subjects discussed should have a customer or service orientation. On rare occasions management may give a quality circle a specific problem to solve.

Pembrokeshire Health Authority has set up 'focus teams' which are designed to achieve results similar to those of quality circles. There is, however, one important difference - unlike quality circles, they address one single issue chosen by management from employee suggestions. These teams are composed of volunteers, and a team leader chosen by a manager. They do not have fixed weekly or monthly meetings but instead meet whenever the members of the team feel it is necessary. A number of minor changes have already been implemented by the authority and new focus teams have been set up. Progress has, however, been slower than management had originally envisaged.

TEAM BRIEFINGS

Team briefings are another popular means for communicating with the workforce so that they are better informed to deal with the public. Eleven of the organisations in our research project use them on a fairly regular basis. Some of these organisations hold team briefings at regular intervals throughout the year, others hold them only when the need arises. They are usually run on the basis of the model provided by the Industrial Society. Each team briefing can usually be divided into two parts: 1) the core brief which deals with corporate and policy matters and 2) local information. The core brief is formulated by the top management of the organisation and is then communicated down to department level. At this level, local issues are added that are of more day-to-day relevance to the staff.

The split between the core brief and the local information varies at different organisations. At Wrekin District Council, the aim is that the briefing should consist of 10 per cent corporate, 20 per cent departmental, and 70 per cent sectional information. It usually takes 48 hours from the initial core brief being formulated by a top manager to the information reaching all levels of staff. Most organisations fix a time limit for the whole process to be completed.

Information Plus Discussion?

Some organisations view team briefing purely as a means of imparting information to employees and do not allow a follow-up discussion. The contrary view is held by British Telecom, which believes that team briefing is a two-way process rather than just a process of 'dumping information'. Most team briefings are aimed at white-collar staff, although the London Borough of Camden has held them for manual workers in connection with compulsory competitive tendering. The borough believes that these team briefings have been very successful in giving information to the workforce, presenting the management point of view, and avoiding industrial action.

However, some organisations have had problems with the trade union reaction to team briefings. For example, because of attempts by Post Office management in some districts to use team briefings to persuade staff to vote against industrial action in 1988, the Union of Communication Workers has adopted a national position of 'passive participation' at team briefings. This means that staff should attend the briefing to listen to management's presentation but not take part in discussing the issues afterwards.

Team Building

Team building has been used by organisations to a far lesser extent than team briefing. One of only two examples found in our research is at Northern Ireland Electricity. Groups of workers are taken away from work for a couple of days to a residential training centre. At the centre, the training department runs workshops which are designed to build team spirit, improve relations within and between teams, and enhance the quality of service provided to the customer. The management believes that team building is a valuable initiative and that it is achieving its aims. Staff reaction has also been favourable.

Team building sessions have also been run by Peterborough Health Authority's Quality Assurance Department. Sessions were held at the Edith Cavell Hospital to help management make the transition from preparing to open a new hospital to actually running it.

STAFF SUGGESTION SCHEMES

Staff suggestion schemes may be another effective method of motivating staff and increasing their sense of involvement in the organisation. They are also, of course, a useful resource for generating ideas to improve service quality and efficiency.

British Airways has recently revamped its staff suggestion scheme, which is now called 'Brainwaves'. In comparison to many other organisations, it offers high monetary rewards to staff who offer good suggestions. During 1988/89, awards totalling more than £92,000 were shared by 476 staff. On a more modest scale, Braintree District Council has launched an 'Enterprise Award Scheme' which offers quarterly cash prizes to employees, and also a small reward, such as a pen or digital clock, for any suggestions made.

Arun District Council runs a suggestion scheme called 'At Your Service', which is open to both staff and the public. Boxes for suggestions from the public are provided in reception areas. For employees there is a form in the staff newsletter. All suggestions are seen by the Chief Executive and are given a personal response.

A more direct method of motivating staff towards accepting the importance of customer care is the 'Employee of the Month' award used at Arun District Council, which was started in 1988. Employees are nominated by their colleagues for particularly outstanding work in the field of customer care and an award is made every month.

HOUSE MAGAZINES AND NEWSPAPERS

House magazines and newspapers are the most common method used to communicate information to staff. These magazines are mostly produced on a monthly basis, but British Airways News is published weekly. Some of these newsheets have recently been revamped as part of a new management approach to staff communication. These publications are often used to interest staff in customer care topics.

Arun District Council encourages its staff to work at achieving 'right first time' customer care through a booklet, 'In The Customer's Shoes', which is issued to all employees. It concentrates on the customer's first contact with the council and gives clear guidance on making these first impressions favourable. It also shows how to deal with complaints and possible aggressive behaviour by council users.

House magazines are also used to overcome communication difficulties within an organisation. At Pembrokeshire Health Authority, for example, where communication problems became apparent from the results of a staff opinion survey, a two page bulletin - 'Update' - was launched to keep staff informed of management and personnel developments. A newspaper, 'The Pembrokeshire Pulse', was also established. In addition, to give staff a better idea of the services offered by Pembrokeshire HA, a video was also made about the history of the first six years of the authority.

EMPLOYEE ATTITUDE SURVEYS

Another key to discovering employee views is the attitude survey. A number of organisations have used this method. In general, the results have generally revealed dissatisfaction with communication channels and relations with management, and complaints about pay.

At Belfast City Hospital, for example, an employee attitude survey revealed staff dissatisfaction with poor communication systems and a lack of management appreciation of their work. The survey also revealed that discontent was highest among administrative and clerical staff. As a result, a number of new measures were introduced and improvements to existing practices made. These included improvements in the quality of staff information bulletins, the introduction of a new 'Quality Assurance Bulletin', and changes to employee induction procedures. The induction sessions now emphasise more firmly the interests of the users of the service. Managers were also briefed on the need to show appreciation of staff efforts.

An attitude survey at Northern Ireland Electricity revealed similar problems. A number of new initiatives were therefore introduced. For example, the staff appraisal system was revised to ensure that it dealt effectively with performance, commitment and development. The survey had shown that the existing staff appraisal scheme was not working properly, primarily because of a lack of management commitment. Finally, 'Flowline', the staff magazine, was redesigned in newspaper style. It is also now delivered to the home of every employee in the hope that the families of employees will identify more closely with the organisation, as well as the employees themselves. Additionally, 'team building' has been introduced, the role of the joint consultative structure for management and unions reviewed, and the staff suggestion scheme revamped.

Employee attitude surveys at Teignbridge District Council, MBS Computer Services, Peterborough Health Authority and Pembrokeshire Health Authority also revealed communication problems. The response rate for staff attitude surveys varies widely but at Braintree District Council it fell to only 29 per cent. A more typical response rate would be between 40 and 50 per cent.

EMPLOYEE APPRAISAL SCHEMES

One means of improving quality of service is to link staff appraisal schemes more closely to customer care. At Braintree District Council, for example, a new system of performance appraisal was introduced in 1988 and is seen as an important means of gaining the support of staff for the authority's customer care policies. The employees' targets, which are mutually agreed between each employee and his or her manager, are linked to the manager's own targets which in turn are linked to those of the Chief Officers and finally to the authority's core values. The appraisal process also identifies the training needs of staff. The system is used for all staff and is also geared towards counselling and personal development.

The Northern Ireland Department of Economic Development has also recently introduced a new staff appraisal system designed to help improve customer services. It is intended that the new system will involve individual members of staff more fully in the appraisal process by requiring them to draft their own job plans and then discuss these with management. Training will also be made available to ensure the effective working of the new appraisal system.

Birmingham City Council carries out performance appraisal for all its senior staff and is planning to extend this to all levels of its organisation. It is intended that performance appraisal will reinforce existing methods of assessing and improving service delivery.

Some health authorities use appraisal only for managers receiving performance-related pay. Peterborough Health Authority, however, is spreading IPR to all staff so that the opportunity will be created for employees to discuss work issues with management. It is also hoped that it will improve communication between employees and management. The authority believes that, although there is no financial benefit, staff will be rewarded by increased job satisfaction, improved communication links with management, and better access to training.

PERFORMANCE-RELATED PAY

Individual performance pay schemes, which can relate reward to quality of service to the public, are also being introduced. For example, the previous incentive scheme for maintenance workers at Gloucestershire County Fire Service gave value to each item of work (changing a wheel, etc). The new scheme will pay the workforce according to the number of vehicles they have actually on the road. In this way a public service orientation is being incorporated into the pay system.

At MBS, the computer company, all employees have been paid on a performance-related basis since the foundation of the company some eight years ago. Annual appraisals are carried out and all increments are performance-related. There is no annual cost-of-living increase; good performance, promotion or applying for a higher grade job are the only options open to employees to increase their incomes. Assessment of performance has recently been extended to include a customer satisfaction requirement and will ultimately contain detailed standards specifications on quality.

STAFF SUPPORT AND DEVELOPMENT

Staff satisfaction is seen by many organisations as a prerequisite for providing a high quality service to the customer. However, improving poor pay and conditions in the public sector may not be easily achieved. Therefore many public service organisations have decided to try to improve the content of their employees' work and relations with management.

Peterborough Health Authority has gone further than most organisations in launching its 'Employee Charter' which lays down clear guidance for managers to follow in their relations with staff. The charter places the demand on managers that they will communicate freely and consult with staff on significant matters that affect them. The health authority has also introduced a 'Positive Action Programme' to back up with action the good intentions of the 'Employee Charter'. This includes the harmonisation of employment conditions, the introduction of equal opportunities policies and staff development, a review of communications, and proposals for improving health and welfare.

Trent Regional Health Authority has also recognised that it needs to satisfy staff desires and interests if it is to introduce effective customer care. To further this end, it has launched 'Caring for the Carers', a funding project designed to develop methods of promoting staff care. Counselling services, for example, have been established for those who dealt with the casualties from the Hillsborough football ground disaster.

Other organisations have stressed the development of staff through increasing the satisfaction they get from their job. For example, Wrekin District Council's performance appraisal system puts the emphasis on staff development rather than assessment of past performance. Individual counselling between manager and employee is used to work out and plan the future career development and training needs of the employee. The aim is to encourage employees to fulfil both the council's objectives and their own aspirations.

This approach was introduced in 1982 and has since led to the development of a widespread secondment policy in which employees are transferred to other departments in order to further their career developments. So far over 300 employees have moved via this method from manual and craft posts to office/supervisory grades. This system can also, of course, serve the council's need for more flexible working patterns.

TRADE UNION AND EMPLOYEE REACTION

Trade union reaction to organisations implementing customer care policies has varied widely. Some innovations, such as quality circles, have attracted little comment from the unions, whereas opposition to team briefings has often been vocal. At Northern Ireland Electricity, trade union shop stewards felt that team briefing undermined their role in communicating the views of management to staff. Team briefings were also opposed at the Post Office.

The London Borough of Camden is experiencing a number of problems with its workforce in its attempts to shift the emphasis of its service provision towards the consumer. The authority is trying to convince its employees that the interests of the producer (council employee) and consumer need not conflict, but if they do, the customer must win. This approach has not, at least in practice, been accepted by the trade unions, as shown in the number of recent disputes (for example in the housing management and building maintenance departments) which directly affected the public.

The council argues that such actions hit the most vulnerable and as such run directly counter to their attempts to develop a customer care strategy. The unions argue that there are many groups of employees, such as meals-on-wheels workers, who have held back from strike action because of the effect on clients. However, at Camden the unions see the quality approach as running directly counter to their interests in effectively threatening their right to strike.

At British Rail, the unions view management's customer care initiatives as a means to save money, rather than deliver higher quality. The proposals are identified with cutting costs and getting the maximum out of people for the minimum of return. However, management hopes that the Quality Through People initiative will convince the 90,000 staff in the lowest grades, where cynicism is most prevalent, of the importance of providing a high quality service. In 1990-91, when the quality initiative will reach the lower levels of the organisation, it is hoped that staff will be persuaded that management is serious in seeking a genuine improvement in quality within the organisation and is not just interested in cost cutting.

More usually, however, unions have reacted more passively to customer care initiatives. Sometimes the reaction has bordered on the cynical. At Northern Ireland Electricity, for example, the words of 'Our Corporate Aim And Objective' were regarded by the unions as not matching management's actions.

At Peterborough Health Authority, the 'Employee Charter' was not enthusiastically received by union representatives on the District Joint Staff Committee. They felt that the charter did not contain sufficient concrete proposals that would improve working conditions for staff. In general, the authority says, trade unions are only interested in customer care policies if they can be shown to also further their members' interests. Some elements of the Positive Action Programme, however, were received more favourably. In particular, the unions supported the abolition of 'clocking in and out' for ancillary workers, the introduction of payment by credit transfer and the establishment of a creche.

Union Consultation Beneficial

If customer care initiatives have no material effect on their members interests, then the unions may take a neutral stance. Conversely, opposition can be overcome if management chooses to consult with the unions over customer care issues. This was the case at the Northern Ireland Department of Economic Development where union anxieties have been overcome by management informing their representatives about any new initiatives. Furthermore, management has given the unions firm assurances that they will be consulted over any proposed changes arising from staff workshop discussions. Again, however, there have been rumblings of cynicism from the unions that quality improvement measures would do little for them.

Staff Reaction

As with the trade unions, cynicism has been a common reaction among staff, at least in the initial stages of customer care development. Often, however, staff can be won over to the idea of quality improvement. At Trent Regional Health Authority, staff working in the North Derbyshire Accident and Emergency Department were initially unwilling to cooperate with the Patient Service Team and its projects. They became more involved, however, when they saw that the team was making genuine progress.

50

The support of staff can also be achieved if employees are closely involved in customer care initiatives. In Glasgow, Royal Mail Letters employees welcomed changes brought about by the introduction of the customer care strategy because they were made to feel part of the process.

Several trade unions have begun to take an interest at national level in improving the quality of services. For example, the National Union of Public Employees (NUPE) has produced a pamphlet for its members which provides concrete examples of improvements achieved in the public services. The union is generally in favour of a 'quality' rather than 'cost-cutting' approach to services, particularly in the context of local government compulsory competitive tendering. Improving the quality of services is therefore seen as a means to combat bids from private contractors.

The TUC has also expressed a strong interest in improving services to the public. Again, the TUC wishes to emphasise the quality of public services as opposed to a simple 'value for money' approach. In 1988 it organised a conference on this topic to which a number of organisations were invited, including the Institute of Personnel Management.

CHANGES TO EMPLOYEES' PAY AND CONDITIONS

Customer care initiatives have so far had little effect on the pay and conditions of employees. Most customer care developments have involved an increase in training, more employee involvement in deciding changes and an improvement in communication channels between management and employees. However, our case studies show that any large scale changes to employees' pay and conditions were only partly the result of customer care initiatives. Changes to pay and conditions at Birmingham City Council, for example, were more the result of the requirements of compulsory competitive tendering, and recruitment and retention difficulties, than customer care initiatives. The council, however, sees some linkage between these changes and attempts to improve the quality of service to the customer.

At West Dorset Health Authority, promoting customer care was perhaps more central to the creation of the Hotel Services Department. The health authority achieved this by combining its ancillary services: catering, domestics, laundry, portering, reception, residence, security and telecommunications into a single department. The department was created initially as a result of drawing up specifications for competitive tendering. The authority felt that a hotel services department would be the most cost efficient way of organising these support services. The decision to combine services, however, was also made because the authority believed that it would improve the quality of service provided to the customer.

The key benefit for the health authority in setting up this new department is the degree of flexibility of its working arrangements which has been achieved. When it was initially set up, training was provided for ancillary workers so that they could work in more than one job. The staff and trade unions were initially opposed to these high levels of labour flexibility required in the new Hotel Services Department. Nevertheless, since the department was established, staff have discovered that flexibility can work in their interests too. Some staff, for example, have been able to move into preferred areas of work that previously had been closed to them. Also, wage levels are protected if staff are moved into a lower paid post.

Similar changes to work flexibility have been implemented at British Telecom with the introduction of 'repatterning' to break down traditional barriers between different areas of work. Previously, if an internal faults engineer was called to a customer's home and diagnosed an external fault, a different category of engineer would be brought in to deal with it. The introduction of 'repatterning', which was accompanied by a pay increase, means that employees will take on a wider, more flexible range of work. Although 'repatterning' is not directly linked to British Telecom's 'Total Quality Management' programme, it clearly has implications for 'customer care'.

In general, private companies are able to devote more resources than public authorities to implementing customer care initiatives. The new flexible working conditions at British Telecom were brought in along with pay increases for the engineers who would have to work to them. A local authority, for example, would probably not have the resources to 'buy' these changes to existing working conditions. Moreover, one result of compulsory competitive tendering in local government and the NHS has been a rationalisation of Direct Service Organisations, with reductions in staffing levels in existing pay and conditions. At Gloucestershire County Council, for example, five out of the six cleaning contracts were won by the authority at the cost of reducing the cleaners' paid working time from 46 to 39 weeks per year.

Furthermore, except when pay and conditions are negatively effected by competitive tendering (unions often have to acquiesce to changes in order to save their members' jobs), national pay and conditions agreements make it difficult for local and health authorities to make major changes in employees' pay and conditions. The linking of customer care initiatives to changes in pay and conditions is generally only possible where some local pay flexibility exists.

At Trent Regional Health Authority there have been no improvements in the pay and conditions of the majority of staff, but the performance-related pay of the top managers was related to the success of the customer care training package 'From Me To You'. Some public service organisations have introduced performance-related pay and also profit-related pay, but these new forms of reward extend to very few employees and are largely concentrated at management level.

One private sector example is British Airways, which has introduced a profit-sharing scheme for all employees. It has been promoted as part of the customer care approach in the belief that a better service to the customer will produce higher profits both for the company and the staff. At the end of 1988-9 this scheme paid out three and a half weeks' salary to the workforce. The bonus should have realised only two and a half weeks' pay, but the company decided to add on an extra week in tribute to the 'first-class job' performed by employees during the year.

Case Studies

ARUN DISTRICT COUNCIL

Arun District Council in West Sussex extends over a largely rural and coastal area which includes the two major towns of Bognor Regis and Littlehampton. Arun's population of approximately 129,000 includes a high proportion (over 30 per cent) of elderly residents. This has encouraged the development of the council's community care. The council is currently Conservative controlled.

The authority employs 650 staff (this number may vary seasonally). These staff are mainly white-collar, as most of the council's direct services, including refuse collection, building maintenance and grounds maintenance, have been contracted out.

Existing services range from housing, environmental amenities, leisure and tourism to community care. The community care service includes the provision of day centres and a 'Community Call Lifeline' telephone system for the elderly. The council has also begun to evolve an economic development strategy for the area. A Business Support Unit has been established as a first point of contact between the council and local businesses.

Unemployment in the area was at one time high, compared with other West Sussex districts, but current employment problems are more likely to relate to skill shortages. In general, Arun sees itself as an 'enabling' council, encouraging other organisations, particularly the private and voluntary sectors, to achieve a higher level of service for the community as a whole.

BACKGROUND

After the last council elections in May 1987, strategy papers were published by the incoming ruling Conservative group. These included the following two principles:

o   an improved awareness of community needs, placing public services in a context of user benefits rather than product features;

o   a new corporate image for the District which stresses the enhanced quality of life in the area and the caring approach of the council.

These principles were incorporated into a report, Working For The Public, which was presented as an 'Action Plan' for getting closer to the customer.

This was produced by the Corporate Unit within the Chief Executive's office in response to a request from councillors for a practical programme of customer care. The report, 'Working For The Public', was approved by the council's Policy and Resources Committee at the end of 1987.

The change in approach called for by the incoming council was necessitated by an increasingly competitive environment and demands for more consumer choice. The elderly, for example, can choose private support services in preference to those offered by the council. The Action Plan presented in 'Working For The Public' (WFP) is aimed at creating a culture 'switched on to the consumer', as opposed to a superficial 'smile campaign'.

The Action Plan is centred on the three key values - 'Quality service', 'Gearing the service to customer needs', and 'Responsiveness to our customers'. Each of these key values is broken down within the report into between four and six key characteristics. These in turn are used as the basis for a number of action points required of specific managers or committees within the council. In this way it is ensured that the Action Plan generates a definite programme of prescribed actions.

At the time the 'Working For The Public' Action Plan was accepted, a steering group was set up, with members drawn from all the council's directorates. This group now meets monthly, in order to oversee the plan. It reports on progress to the council's management team of Chief Officers and to the Policy and Resources committee.

RESTRUCTURING FOR CHANGE

The WFP programme itself has not brought about any changes in the council's organisation, but considerable restructuring over the last few years has resulted in the creation of four new multi-disciplinary departments, Environment and Leisure, Finance and Administration, Planning and Economic Development, and Housing and Community Care. This reorganisation is aimed at making Arun both more effective and more efficient, thus achieving better customer care.

The strategy behind the changes was developed during the previous (1983-1987) administration, which had a competitive and business approach, concentrating on 'value for money' within the council. This led to an overall tendency to move resources towards the 'sharp end' of the council's business. The emphasis here has been on the accountability of individual managers for their particular spheres of activity in a context of cost centres and business plans. Directorates operate on a four-year timescale, within which they have to produce yearly action plans, giving concrete guidelines for the future progress of the service.

IMPLEMENTING 'WORKING FOR THE PUBLIC'

The structural reorganisation had already been completed by 1987 when Working For The Public was launched. The involvement of staff at all levels within the council was seen as crucial to the strategy, and the WFP group therefore set about establishing a system of training and development of staff in customer care.

Training Sessions

Training was carried out initially through a three-week programme on ten half-day sessions involving all staff within the authority. The aim of these sessions was to make staff aware of the WFP approach and to draw out their suggestions. Beginning with a 'scene-setter' from the Chief Executive, in which he explained the basis for the WPF programme in terms of increased competition and consumer choice, the sessions went on to show a video, 'A Passion For Excellence', based on the Peters and Waterman book. Finally, group discussions took place in which staff looked at what the council as a whole should be doing and at what they themselves could do to improve customer care. The outcome of each session was intended to be a personalised action plan produced by each employee.

The group discussions resulted in over four hundred suggestions, ranging from introducing sliding doors instead of the heavy front doors in the council's reception area to putting notices on the lifts giving the location of various departments. The WFP group has undertaken to look at all suggestions and report those seen as feasible to the management team of Chief Officers. Where suggestions are not seen as feasible, the group will, in any case, report back to the individual and explain the decision, as it is seen as important not to undermine motivation.

A number of suggestions have already been implemented at relatively low cost. These include the sliding doors, improved interview rooms in reception, and the provision of umbrellas for the open walkway between the council's swimming pool and the sports centre.

The result of both the group discussions and the individual action plans are followed up within directorates by the WFP group representatives. Part of this monitoring process is to make sure individuals are given help in implementing their action plans, as well as ensuring that the initiative as a whole does not end with the half-day session.

Further Training And Communications Initiatives

One point which emerged very strongly from the initial group sessions on customer care was the need to improve induction training so that employees could be better informed about the activities of the council as a whole. On this basis the WFP group has now set up a rolling programme of induction courses which take place once a month. In this way every new employee receives induction training within a month of starting work. These sessions emphasise the corporate culture of the organisation, of which customer care is a central aspect.

Staff Awareness Sessions

In order to promote awareness and communication among existing staff, the group has also introduced a series of special 'Staff Awareness Sessions'. These concentrate on particular issues of relevance to the council, and are held at lunchtimes so that attendance is both voluntary and practicable. Sessions so far have concentrated on issues such as the community charge, a major development scheme on the Arun riverside, and - planned for late 1989 - the opening of a new Day Centre for the elderly in Bognor (for this session, staff will be encouraged to visit the centre).

These Staff Awareness Sessions are seen as promoting customer care through helping staff to become better informed in their dealings with customers.

Front-Line Staff

A further initiative has been in the area of 'front-line' staff who deal directly with the customer. The WFP Action Plan recognises that such staff have often been undervalued in the past, a fact often reflected in their low gradings and low status. To give such employees increased status and support, the WFP group has set up a self-help group made up of 'front-liners'.

The first action taken by this group was to give itself a name - the 'First Impressions Group'. The group then set itself up on a regular basis, meeting once a month. The council's Public Relations Officer, the member of staff ultimately responsible for customer care, attends the meetings to make sure that the points raised will be acted on. Staff attend the meetings from different areas on a rotating basis. This group has provided useful feedback on issues such as telephone responses in internal departments.

Communicating With The Customer

Telephone technique in general is taught on all training courses, including during induction, and the WFP group is now launching a poster campaign on the theme of 'Own That Phone', encouraging staff to pick up a ringing telephone and 'own' the problem, even if the call is not for them. The basis of this approach is that no member of staff can look to others to solve a problem - it is the responsibility of staff as a whole to consider the customer.

A major initiative in 1989 in communicating more effectively with the customer has been the use of the Plain English Campaign to carry out an audit of publications within the authority. Many of the council's standard letters and leaflets are written in bureaucratic language and these are now being rigorously examined. Staff who produce these leaflets are now being urged to write more clearly, and Plain English training is being arranged for all key staff.

Staff have also been issued with a booklet, 'In The Customer's Shoes'. Using cartoons and vivid language, the booklet examines the customer's first interaction with the council. It gives guidance on making these first impressions favourable and also shows how to deal with complaints and possibly aggressive behaviour by council users.

Another method of improving both staff and customer 'feedback' is the authority's suggestion scheme, 'At Your Service', which is open to both employees and members of the public. Suggestion boxes are provided in reception areas. All contributions are seen by the Chief Executive and are given a personal response. The authority is trying to create an environment in which it is extremely easy to make suggestions.

Setting up effective employee/customer consultation groups is a central aim of the Action Plan. Three new consultation panels are planned, which will include key sections of the community - service users, representative groups and council staff - to establish a two-way channel of communication.

Communications With Staff

To keep staff informed on customer care, the WFP group puts out a regular monthly newsletter, but this is seen as a 'stopgap' prior to the publication of a staff journal to be launched shortly. In addition to a survey run by the newsletter, staff informants or 'stringers' have been used within departments to convey opinions on the content of, and provide articles for, the new journal. In this way the journal is seen as being 'by staff, for staff'.

Others methods of communicating with staff include Team Briefings, which have until now been carried out within departments. The WFP group is currently examining the effectiveness of these briefings. All standards of consultation and communication, such as team briefings, quality circles and 'service days' (in which staff are brought together with management to consider ways of improving the service) are being reviewed in order to come up with fresh ways of gaining the motivation and involvement of the workforce. The main priority is seen as keeping up the impetus towards change and avoiding the feeling among the staff of 'we've been through all this before'.

A customer care award is another initiative aimed at boosting employee confidence and involvement. Originally entitled 'Employee Of The Month', the scheme, begun in 1988, has now been given a more distinctively customer-related emphasis. Each month an employee, who has been nominated by colleagues, councillors or members of the public as having achieved particularly outstanding customer care, is presented with an award - for example, the last recipient was the Senior Welfare Officer, in recognition of her work within the community. This scheme was at first greeted with some cynicism by employees but is now seen as valuable.

PRIORITISING THE CONSUMER

The council is particularly keen to eliminate the 'us' and 'them' attitude among employees in their dealings with the public. In budgeting, for example, a priority budgeting system has been introduced in which departments are asked to look at services and identify them as either essential or desirable. The aim is to question whether the department should carry on providing the service or whether there should be a change in provision. Departments are also asked to consider whether their services are always angled to what the customer wants and whether there are emerging consumer interests which should be catered for.

The WFP Action Plan also emphasises the need for market research. Consumer research through MORI or a similar organisation is one option currently being assessed. An initial survey was carried out through a special edition of 'Arun News', the council newsletter delivered to every household. This was followed by a major survey of service provision, looking at trends into the 1990s, carried out for the council by the Henley Management Centre. This provided the material for the document, 'Arun Trends', issued by the council and will also be used as the basis for investigating the needs of particular sectors.

The council has also carried out a survey entitled 'Are You Being Served?', which arose from the initial customer care training sessions. At these sessions, some staff raised questions about possible changes in opening hours for council offices and accessibility of council meetings. This survey, which was based on a one per cent sample of the district's population (1,200), showed a rather low level of awareness by residents of council provision. For example, 14 per cent of the sample did not know the name of their district authority, and 59 per cent had never contacted the council. Asked if they would visit the Arun Civic Centre (Town Hall) if it were to open on a Saturday morning, only 27 per cent said yes. On the more positive side, 37 per cent of those questioned said they would be interested in attending a council meeting and ten per cent had already done so. Arun News was a popular source of information about the council, with 52 per cent of the sample having read it (local papers were the prime source with 84 per cent).

Particular sections have also carried out their own surveys on customer satisfaction, for example a customer survey to test satisfaction with the refuse collection service. The Housing Department has integrated customer 'feedback' into its ordinary working practices by talking to those tenants whose properties are being improved. Tenants are asked about whether they are happy with the service and, for example, if they would prefer bath or shower facilities.

Finally, the WFP group is considering carrying out a 'Customer Care Audit', in which a questionnaire relating to the effectiveness of the service will be issued to heads of departments. This would be a modified version of a

Customer Audit questionnaire used by another authority, and is still at a pilot stage within Arun. Despite the need for feedback, the council recognises that it is important not to bombard its service users with pieces of paper. It is also concerned to report all survey results back to respondents.

IMPACT ON EMPLOYEES

This customer-centred approach has not brought about any major changes in basic terms and conditions for most of Arun's employees. Performance-related pay has been introduced for senior and middle management, but this has been more a response to recruitment and retention difficulties than a result of the WFP programme. The Chief Executive would like to see the system extended further down the organisation, and this may lead to some quality criteria being integrated into performance assessment. The impact of customer care initiatives on most employees' terms and conditions has been more in the area of working patterns than pay. Lunchtime openings for 'front-line' service offices were introduced in 1988, along with flexitime. The WFP group is now looking at whether flexitime is being worked for the benefit of customers as well as staff.

Saturday and late night opening are being looked at in the context of the 'Are You Being Served?' survey, in order to determine the extent of customer demand for such changes. It is recognised that customers may prefer a large number of access points for services in remote areas rather than longer opening hours at a central point. An extension of services of this kind has already been provided in Bognor, with a new area office being opened on the lines of a 'One-Stop Shop', computer-linked to Arun. A branch office has also been opened on a trial basis for one afternoon a week in the small village of Barnham.

Any major step, such as Saturday opening of offices, would have to be discussed with the trade unions, whose views will be integrated into any moves made to change working hours and other conditions.

CREATING A CORPORATE CULTURE

The council sees its Working For The Public action plan as its major means to motivate staff, rather than a specific set of core values. Core values are being considered, although the council says these will not be 'tablets of stone'.

Measures Of Success

While the council considers it has achieved a great deal over the first eighteen months of its strategy, there is still some way to go. The need to serve other council departments as 'internal' customers, with the same attention as they serve the public, is taking some time to get across.

One difficulty in accurately measuring progress is identified by the council. This is that the more that council services are opened up to public scrutiny, the more complaints are likely to be made. On the other hand, the absence of complaint need not be taken to mean that consumers are satisfied. The council is encouraged by the obvious improvements that have taken place in areas like reception, and the fact that employees are increasingly talking about customer care.

Cost Implications

The WFP group itself has not been given its own budget, and therefore has had to persuade other directorates to make money available for its initiatives. For example, Finance and Administration was asked to provide the money for the new sliding doors in reception, and for the improved interview 'cells' (where enlarging the rooms and providing better lighting gave rise to a bill of £200). The training budget within Personnel was redirected to provide money for the customer care programme, and the funding for corporate publications comes out of the Public Relations budget. If all these sums were added up, the council suggests the total 'might be quite considerable'. However the WFP group has worked at redirecting existing resources towards the customer, rather than creating new resources. This has helped to keep costs down.

BRAINTREE DISTRICT COUNCIL

Braintree District Council in Essex is responsible for an area of 236 square miles and a population of 117,500. The north of the district is mainly rural but the south contains the three urban centres of Braintree, Witham and Halstead. The council is currently Conservative controlled.

The council currently employs 545 APT&C staff and 296 'skilled/operational' staff (the term given to manual workers after a recent harmonisation exercise) although the actual establishment size for both groups is higher. The council is having some difficulty in filling professional vacancies, particularly in the planning, environmental services and computing departments.

The council provides technical, planning, community, environmental and housing services in addition to its internal support services, such as finance and personnel. Technical services, such as refuse collection, have recently been brought together in a Direct Services Organisation, called 'Braintree District Commercial Services', which has a commercial contractor/client relationship with the council.

BACKGROUND

Braintree has been firmly committed to 'customer care' since the appointment of its current Chief Executive in 1984, when the slogan 'Braintree Means Business' and the council's core values were introduced. The area was beginning to experience economic decline with the withdrawal of a major local employer from the district and the council perceived a need for a new management strategy based on improved accountability and delivery of services. At the same time an economic development strategy was introduced which emphasised the creation of the right conditions for new private investment, centred on small industrial units. The two strategies began to merge and the phrase 'Braintree Means Business' became a vehicle for major organisational changes within the council.

A number of moves towards a more corporate, customer-oriented organisation were introduced during this period, including:

o   Increased emphasis on improving service standards, with target setting, monitoring, and business plans established in each department.

o   A system of annual reporting linked to business plans, in which each department was established as a cost centre.

o   The extension of the existing performance appraisal system to manual workers and business plan targets were incorporated into this system.

o   Development of income generation activities, eg marketing the expertise of the training department on a commercial basis.

o   The establishment of Braintree District Commercial Services as an autonomous Direct Services Organisation.

o   The increased surveying of public attitudes on the council's activities through opinion polls.

An important part of Braintree's customer care policy is the marketing of the council's services to local business. Recent appointments to the authority include a new Marketing Manager and Public Relations officer in the attempt to develop links with commercial clients. The council says its dominant values are efficiency and value for money . Cost centres are being established in each department with strictly controlled budgets. The main emphasis is to provide better and more cost-effective services to ratepayers. The council's original core values, which are now seen as 'too jargonistic' are being refined to centre on the three key words, 'Quality, Service and Customer'.

A new management structure designed to sharpen accountabilities and to reduce the barriers to communication which tend to occur at middle management level, is now being introduced. Most skilled and operational grades or basic grade clerical workers, for example, would have to go through five or six management tiers to reach Chief Officer level. It is felt that many of these employees have no real need of direct supervision, and the number of levels can therefore be reduced to four - operational/administrative support, technical/professional, senior management and Chief Officers. A senior management group has been set up to oversee the reorganisation, which is intended to be completed within two years. Any job changes will be dealt with through redeployment.

PERSONNEL IMPLICATIONS

Training

The council's policy has a number of implications for the personnel function - in training; recruitment and selection; induction of new staff; employee appraisal; and employee communications.

Training is seen as a key element in promoting the council's customer-oriented corporate culture. The amount spent on training is already approaching the council's target of two per cent of the total staffing budget. Training programmes have now moved away from the traditional courses on professional enhancement and technical short courses. In their place, a twin track approach has been adopted, in which senior officers are trained in promoting a customer care perspective, while employees dealing with the public are given courses on customer relations and telephone techniques. These latter courses are now being extended to repair and maintenance staff.

All training courses are linked to the council's core values, with an emphasis on persuading staff to see themselves as serving a customer, rather than simply carrying out departmental functions. The training courses themselves are monitored and reviewed along the same lines as other internal support services.

Recruitment And Selection

The authority has spent three years reshaping its recruitment and selection policy to ensure that it contributes to the 'customer care' approach. A high priority is also put on the induction of new employees who, after an initial introduction to the organisation, are given a follow-up address by the Chief Executive on the importance of customer care.

Performance Appraisal

A new system of performance appraisal, introduced in 1988, is seen by the council as an important means to communicate the authority's customer care approach. The system, in which all staff are appraised at least once a year, is linked to the business plan targets set for each department under the council's new structure. Manager and employee mutually agree the employee's targets for the year. The employee's targets are linked to the departmental manager's, which in turn are linked to those of the Chief Officers and the authority's core values and policy objectives.

Employee Communications

In other respects, the authority's methods of communicating with and consulting staff are described by the Chief Executive as 'a mixture of formal and informal'. The Chief Executive takes a personal interest in communicating with the workforce and spends as much time as possible talking to staff, including holding coffee morning discussions and going out with refuse and drainage crews.

The council puts out a six-weekly newsletter, which is now being supplemented by many departments with their own newsletter. All Chief Officers are required to organise departmental management teams and hold team briefings on a regular basis. These are seen as a two-way process in which employee comments and suggestions are as important as 'top-down' information. Quality circles exist on a small scale within the Commercial Services department, but so far these have not led to any changes in working practices. The authority has now begun a process of 'lunchtime learn-ins', at which a senior member of staff holds a briefing session on a particular service.

In addition, a suggestion scheme known as the 'Enterprise Award Scheme' has been launched, with incentives. Employees receive a small reward, such as a pen or a digital clock, for any suggestions but there is also a major quarterly prize.

A working group of officers has also been set up to discuss the implications of compulsory competitive tendering and the progress of services coming up for tender.

Employee Attitude Surveys

The authority has carried out a number of internal employee surveys to monitor how staff are responding to its customer care initiatives. The latest of these has been disappointing in securing only a 29 per cent response rate and may indicate that a number of communication blockages still exist within the organisation. A team of Chief Officers has now assessed the results of the survey and authorised a number of changes as a consequence. The survey will be repeated shortly on the basis of a ten-point checklist to monitor any improvements.

HARMONISATION STRATEGY

A major recent initiative aimed at linking changes in the pay structure to the corporate culture of the organisation is the council's new harmonisation agreement for its 300 skilled and operational workers. All manual worker bargaining groups are now merged into a single pay structure consisting of a 38-point pay spine and bonus earnings have been consolidated.

Each of the former manual grades is allocated a number of points on the spine, and progression through the grades will be based on performance appraisal according to a system of 'factor marking'. The factors used in the assessment, which is carried out jointly between manager and employee, include workload, achievement of individual and group targets, flexibility and commitment to customer orientation. This method of pay enhancement was chosen by the workforce in preference to an original proposal for a profit-sharing scheme. The similarity of the scheme to the performance appraisal system for white-collar workers underlines the council's objective of ultimately achieving a 'one-employee' workforce in which traditional divisions between manual and non-manual workers are overcome. Symbolic of this is the decision to give manual workers the title 'skilled and operational staff'.

The introduction of payment by credit transfer has yet to be agreed, but both sides have undertaken to resolve this over the next three years. Other changes in terms and conditions, for example extending the working week or introducing annualised hours, are under consideration for individual service groups.

Performance-related Pay

Performance-related pay has also been introduced for all second and third grade officers, and there are plans to extend it further down the organisation.

At present the system is optional for existing staff, but new staff at these levels will have no choice in whether their pay is linked to performance or not. This change is seen as a means to improve employee motivation at this level. It is emphasised that the genuine measurement of improved performance, according to the corporate objectives of the organisation, has to be the basis for salary enhancement.

EMPLOYEE RESPONSE

Motivation and job satisfaction amongst the workforce is considered to be generally high. However, one issue which has recently emerged among administrative and clerical staff is the increasing pressure of work caused by the council's developing structure of business plans, departmental targets, cost centres etc. All these policies require a considerable level of monitoring for effective implementation, and this is added on to employees' normal work routines. A new initiative requiring employees to fill in time sheets has now been introduced in some departments. This is necessary for costing services in relation to other departments, as every department now has to justify its own costs in relation to the overall organisation.

While this approach ties in with the corporate objectives of the council and has a strong bearing on its consumer orientation, setting and monitoring the cost and quality of standards now required puts an increased burden on administrative staff. However, overall there has not been any major reaction by staff against these developments.

COST IMPLICATIONS AND MEASURES OF SUCCESS

The cost of Braintree's customer care initiatives has so far been kept largely within existing budgets, and their success is assessed as high on a number of indicators. These include:

o   Staff turnover, at eight per cent, is claimed to be one of the lowest in the South East;

o   Good quality short lists when recruiting for posts; and

o   High ratings in the recent MORI customer opinion poll.

WREKIN DISTRICT COUNCIL

Wrekin Council in Shropshire covers an area of 114 square miles and a population of 136,000. Two thirds of the area are rural but the district also includes Telford New Town (which has 85 per cent of the population and is growing at a rate of 3,000 a year). The authority employs 1,300 staff, of which half are counted as white-collar and half manual - many previously manual grades such as vehicle technicians, wardens, and catering workers are now termed staff as part of a policy of gradual harmonisation.

In 1981 the Council underwent a re-organisation which reduced the number of departments from eight to five. These now consist of three main service departments (Operational Services, Housing and Leisure and Community Services), two supporting departments (Finance and Administration and Planning and Environmental Services) and a small number of specialist units. The Council currently has a Labour majority.

BACKGROUND

The council has had a customer service orientation since the early 1980s, when a new Chief Executive and a new Personnel Manager were appointed. In addition to the re-organisation of the council's structure, which itself led to more emphasis on customer services, the council has benefited from a supportive group of councillors committed to a service orientation.

The customer initiatives are based on two sources: the writings of Peters and Waterman in 'In Search Of Excellence', and subsequent publications by The Institute of Local Government and the Local Government Training Board, in particular 'Getting Closer To The Customer' by John Stewart and Michael Clarke.

At the same time, the council has developed a reputation locally as a model employer, which is seen as directly linked to the provision of high-quality services to the customer. Conditions of service provided for employees of Wrekin Council since its inception in 1974 include free life assurance, a nine-day fortnight, and paternity leave. There have also been moves towards single status or harmonisation.

The Council's moves towards customer care are based on a recognition that the provision of high-quality service requires a high level of employee involvement. This has led to the development and promotion of a set of core values, - 'Quality, Caring and Fairness' or 'QCF'. These values were devised in 1983 by a group representing a cross-section of the Wrekin Council workforce. They are promoted mainly through training, a central element in reinforcing the corporate culture. Other elements are communication and staff development (contrasted with the more usual performance appraisal).

In addition, relating more directly to the customer, the council has launched an extensive programme of research into residents' attitudes towards council services, using the results in many cases to modify these services.

NEW COMMERCIAL APPROACH

The Council is now developing a commercial side to its activities through the organisation of training seminars on a fee-paying basis, recruitment consultancy work, etc. The Personnel Unit has set itself an income target of £20,000 pa from these sources, and marketing activities are being developed in a number of departments. These will shortly be pulled together with the appointment of a marketing specialist.

This commercial approach is balanced by a strong community orientation on the part of the council. The main indication of its MORI survey of residents' attitudes was a need for more accessibility to the council. As a result, Wrekin has embarked on a decentralisation programme in which 'Local Shops' are being established in High Street locations away from the main Telford shopping centre and council offices. These are seen as 'a tangible example of what we are doing on the customer front'.

Unlike many other authorities, Wrekin Council has not established any independent Direct Services Organisation to cater for its technical activities, such as refuse collection and grounds maintenance. The council sees its starting point as 'wanting to provide jobs and services by direct labour' and has already won the contract for its public cleaning services, first on the list of those to be put out to tender under the 1988 Local Government Act.

PERSONNEL IMPLICATIONS

Wrekin District Council's starting point in achieving its corporate customer care approach is its position as a 'model employer'. This is summed up by the personnel manager as: 'We give our employees the best, we expect the best back from them'.

Beyond this, the customer care approach has been pursued through four employee strategies:

Reinforcement Of Corporate Identity Through Core Values

The group of employees who originally devised Wrekin's core values have become the basis of a group which is now working with Bath University to re-examine Wrekin's corporate culture in the light of the many changes affecting local government.

Recruitment And Induction

Recruitment of the 'right' people is seen as essential in order to further the council's corporate objectives. A wide range of assessment techniques have therefore been introduced for both senior and junior level posts. These include psychometric testing as well as a range of activities tailored to the post in hand - for example a candidate for the post of principal environmental health officer might be asked to present a report on the key environmental issues facing local government in the 1990s. An exercise is also used in which interviewees are asked to sort through a collection of papers and initiate responses. Group discussions are set up on the basis of bringing together a number of points of view which then have to be integrated into a group consensus.

While conventional measures, such as interview performance, qualifications, references etc are taken into account in the recruitment process, Wrekin is concerned to supplement these by forms of assessment which simulate the activities involved in the job itself. The authority's recruitment policies for both senior and junior posts are seen as more strenuous and rigorous than those of most others. Recruitment to the more senior posts can take three days and considerable time is also spent on recruitment to junior levels.

Selected employees are then provided with a comprehensive first day induction programme, 'Welcome to Wrekin', with introductory talks by the Chief Executive and Personnel Manager, and through a video. Qualifications in themselves are seen as less important than acceptance and endorsement of these values.

Staff Development Scheme

This term covers a form of performance appraisal for council employees which emphasises staff development rather than assessment. Individual counselling of an employee by his or her manager is used as the basis for working out future career development and training needs. The aim is to encourage employees to fulfil both the council's objectives and their own aspirations.

This approach, known as Development Review, was introduced in 1982 and has since led to a policy of secondment of employees to other departments in order to further their career development. So far over 300 employees have moved via this method, including many from manual and craft posts to office/supervisory positions. This system can also, of course, serve the council's need for flexibility in its workforce.

Training And Development

The council has always placed a strong emphasis on training, but this was given added impetus in 1986 with the appointment of a Training and

Development Officer and the provision of a well-equipped training centre. The centre has introduced three major initiatives:

(a) **Service Days.** Each section of employees spends a day in the training centre during which they jointly examine the services they provide, identify barriers to achieving high-quality and prepare action plans for improved service delivery.

b) **'Core Days' On Caring For Our Customers.** Every employee is required to attend a day's training on customer needs, which is then followed by a training programme specific to his or her department's services. Training within the department concerned may then be continuous; for example, the housing department organises and runs courses on the problems of homeless people and on welfare and housing benefit. These take place during the hour and a half the department is closed every week - one hour for training and half an hour for team briefings. Similarly, in Leisure and Community Services there are courses in reception techniques, customer care courses for pool attendants, and marketing courses with a customer care component. Some of the elements in the departmental modules may arise out of suggestions made by employees in the original 'core day' - for example many have called for a longer session on awkward customers.

(c) **Communication Package.** This consists of advice on telephone courtesy, letter writing, and other communications skills relating to the customer.

The Service Days have been particularly beneficial in bringing about a positive employee identification with the council's objectives on service delivery.

COMPOSITION OF WORKFORCE

The proportion of women employed within the council is approximately 35 per cent, with women concentrated in the lower grades. Only a small proportion of women are employed in senior posts and there are none in the two most senior tiers of the council. On race issues the council is also perceived as having so far failed to redress the balance. The representation of ethnic minority workers within the council is nowhere near the four per cent proportion in the local population.

However, the council is committed to redressing this problem and the Personnel Sub-Committee has recently approved a report containing proposals for a code practice on recruitment and selection, a revised equal opportunities policy statement and specific strategies for women including training, career breaks and help with childcare arrangements.

However, the council feels that it has achieved some success in employing people with disabilities. It has won two awards under the 'Fit For Work' scheme, and this is seen as a 'spur to further action', rather than as grounds for complacency.

The council's equal opportunities policy is also related to effective service delivery. The authority argues that, in an organisation which provides services to the community, these services are best provided by a workforce which broadly reflects the community it serves.

MOTIVATING THE WORKFORCE

Communications with the workforce are seen as a central part of the council's strategy. The two major means of communication are team briefings and the weekly employee newsletter.

In the last two to three years, team briefings have been introduced 'from top to bottom' of the organisation. Meetings take place weekly on a cascading basis. This process begins every Tuesday morning with a meeting of Chief Officers. This meeting may centre on two or three items of corporate information of interest to all employees, for example the news that the council has just won an in-house tender. This is known as 'core brief' information.

This information is then transmitted down to departmental level, where further meetings will include additional information on specific departmental items. This information is then passed down to each section where much more detailed information is added by the section head for a comparatively small group of employees. By the time the team briefing reaches this level, the aim is that the information should be roughly 70 per cent sectional, 20 per cent departmental and 10 per cent corporate. The entire team briefing takes 48 hours from the time of the first Chief Officer/Directorate meetings to individual employees being informed.

The weekly newsletter, distributed to each of the 1,300 council employees, reinforces this information and the ideas put across in the team briefings. It also provides a forum for advertising job vacancies and providing corporate news. Employee/management working groups may also meet on an ad hoc basis to discuss particular issues, such as the competitive tendering of a service.

PAY AND CONDITIONS

A system of 'stabilised pay' was introduced by the council five years ago as part of a move towards the eventual harmonisation of manual and staff conditions. This is also directed towards reinforcing the council's corporate values. Stabilised earnings were introduced between 1983 and 1985 to overcome fluctuations in weekly pay and some of the bonus disputes which had caused severe industrial relations problems. Every manual/craft employee now receives a regular weekly wage, inclusive of any bonus (limited overtime is still necessary in some cases). The amount paid is based on the employee's average earnings over the previous twelve months.

Similarly, full pay (including average bonus) is now paid for all sick leave, another local benefit introduced in 1983. Since this time overall sickness absence has declined.

Staff status on non-manual pay and conditions, has now been given to a number of groups, including vehicle maintenance workers, building supervisors and wardens. The ultimate objective is total harmonisation across the whole range of conditions of service, for example bringing down the manual workers' 39-hour week to the 36 hours worked by non-manuals. Annualised hours have already been introduced in grounds maintenance in order to prepare for competitive tendering, on the basis of 45 hours over five days during seven months of the year and 31 hours over four days in the remaining five months, all at plain time rates.

There have been no compulsory redundancies within the organisation as a result of compulsory competitive tendering (CCT), but the workforce in cleansing has been reduced through natural wastage in order to prepare for the process of tendering. Competitive tendering is not seen as the impetus behind the council's strategy of improving services, as this process of organisational change began long before the onset of CCT. It is acknowledged that no organisation can provide exceptional customer care overnight. Wrekin's strategy has been built up over a number of years and has been based firstly on its belief in the importance of employee involvement, resulting in the conscious effort to become a 'model employer' and, secondly, the philosophy of 'excellence', in relation to customer care. The council considers that the two are inextricably linked.

COST IMPLICATIONS AND MEASURES OF SUCCESS

The council has never used a separate budget in order to fund its customer care initiatives - all projects have been managed within existing resources. The main cost implications have been in the particularly time-consuming training and communication programmes which cut into the working time of staff. However any such costs have been felt to be well worth it. The council quotes increased employee involvement and the consumer satisfaction shown in the results of the annual Residents' Attitude Surveys carried out by the authority as proof of success. Individual departments such as the housing department have also issued questionnaires to clients which again show a high level of satisfaction.

PEMBROKESHIRE DISTRICT HEALTH AUTHORITY

Pembrokeshire Health Authority is situated in the south-western corner of Wales and has a resident population of 111,000. The health authority was created in April 1982 with the division of Dyfed HA into Pembrokeshire HA and East Dyfed HA.

The major hospital in the district is Withybush General Hospital in Haverfordwest which has a capacity of 368 beds. The smaller South Pembrokeshire Hospital has 57 beds, the Mental Handicap Unit 32 beds, the Geriatric Day Hospital 25 beds and the Tenby Cottage Hospital 16 beds. Most services are provided in the district but some, including dermatology and ophthalmology, are provided by the neighbouring East Dyfed Health Authority.

Pembrokeshire Health Authority employs 1,833 people, including 897 nurses, 360 ancillaries, 232 administrative and clerical staff, and 163 professional and technical staff.

BACKGROUND

Between 1982 and 1987, the authority carried out a number of management reforms to improve the efficiency of hospital services, including the changes required by competitive tendering exercises. Both cleaning and catering services contracts were won by the in-house workforce but at the expense of redundancies, lower pay and reduced standards of working conditions.

By 1987, management was aware of staff disenchantment with the changes of the preceding five years. Management also realised that these changes did not reflect a concern for people. Indeed it had 'become increasingly difficult to get centrally-led initiatives to be accepted and enthusiastically implemented'. In an attempt to lift staff morale and also to provide a better service for patients, the authority decided on two programmes of action. It set up a working party to review the authority's management structure and instituted a 'Quality Assurance Project'.

The working party looking at the authority's management structure was set up in 1987 and included a consultant from the King's Fund College, the NHS management training centre. The conclusions of the working party led to the establishment of two new General Manager posts for the Withybush General Hospital and Community Services. These managers would share access to central personnel, finance and planning support.

To run the 'Quality Assurance Project', a steering group was set up, chaired by the district treasurer, and a former British Airways 'customer service' manager was brought in as a consultant. The object of the project was to 'improve staff morale and provide a better service for the patients'.

STAFF OPINION SURVEY

The steering group's first decision was to commission a survey of employee opinions from the Arbitration, Conciliation and Advisory Service (ACAS).

Follow up interviews with some of the respondents were also planned to gather more detailed information. All trade unions in the authority were invited to participate in organising the survey and representatives of NUPE, NALGO, COHSE, RCN and RCM sat on the joint union and management working party. Only ASTMS (now MSF) and the craft unions chose not to support the survey.

Some 42 per cent of employees returned the confidential questionnaires and the results of the survey were published in December 1987. These showed that staff were dissatisfied in three main areas: communications and consultation; induction and training; and pay and conditions. With the exception of pay and conditions, which are largely beyond the authority's control (although staff did express unhappiness with the lack of social facilities and with heavy workloads), the other areas of dissatisfaction could be tackled. The authority therefore decided to respond immediately to the communications problems and to establish a longer term programme to improve quality.

COMMUNICATIONS STRATEGY

To overcome the communications problems highlighted by the survey, four responses were immediately initiated. To keep staff informed of management and personnel developments a two page bulletin, 'Update', was launched. The first issue dealt with the results of the ACAS survey, while the second issue outlined a new management arrangement. A staff newspaper, 'The Pembrokehshire Pulse', was also established. To give staff a better idea of the services offered by Pembrokeshire HA, a video about the history of the first six years of the authority was made. Finally, monthly team briefings based on the Industrial Society model, were instituted for hospital management.

'ASPIRING TO EXCELLENCE'

The name chosen for the programme that grew from the 'Quality Assurance Project' was 'Aspiring to Excellence'. A report of the same name was published in December 1988. A logo based on outline drawings of employees was introduced to emphasise that 'excellence is achieved through, and for, people'. This logo appears on all material published for 'Aspiring to Excellence'.

Earlier, in September 1988, a workshop for 80 of the authority's managers had been run in order to generate management commitment to the 'Aspiring to Excellence' programme. This workshop also led to a series of management projects that covered: waiting times at clinics, staff appraisal, a check list for strategic reviewing of services, a 'listening manager' module, and a 'who do I go to' guide.

The key to the whole 'Aspiring to Excellence' programme was a series of one-day staff events from October to December 1988, to which all employees were invited. The events attempted to:

o   Review the past and set challenges for the future;

o   Introduce the concept of 'the customer';

o   Review communications and systems to improve quality; and

o   Generate improved teamwork by breaking down inter-departmental barriers.

Participation was voluntary but over 90 per cent of the staff attended. The programme itself contained audio-visual material and a series of workshop sessions on the communications, customer, human and systems 'factors' in the health authority. The events were introduced by consultants but 12 staff from different areas of the authority ran the sessions. At the end of each event the District General Manager faced an interview from the professional presenter using questions that had been raised by staff during the day.

At the workshop sessions the staff were asked to come up with their own ideas to improve the authority's performance. These ideas were collected and collated for possible implementation in the authority. As a result of the ideas expressed at these 'staff events', and the findings of the ACAS survey, the authority's induction programme was revitalised. A course called 'Foundations', run on two half-days (complete with an induction information pack), is now available for all new employees.

The cost of 'Aspiring to Excellence' was shared by the NHS Training Authority (NHSTA) and the Manpower Consultancy Service, an organisation sponsored by the Welsh Office. As a condition of receiving NHSTA funding, Pembrokeshire HA will hold two conferences to present reports on the implementation and effects of 'Aspiring to Excellence'.

'FOCUS TEAMS'

'Focus teams' were established in November 1988 to follow up some of the ideas generated by the series of staff events held under the 'Aspiring to Excellence' programme. These are designed to achieve similar results as quality circles but with one important difference: they address one single issue. These teams are composed of volunteers, and a team leader chosen by a manager. The manager is also expected to provide information and resource support to the team. They do not have fixed weekly or monthly meetings, instead they meet whenever the members of the team feel it is necessary. Six issues were chosen by management from employee suggestions for the first focus teams. These were:

o   Staff uniforms

o   Ambulance services

o   Creche facilities

o   Accommodation and arrangements for relatives

o   Medical Records Department

o   Withybush General Hospital corridor facilities.

The focus teams reported their initial findings in January 1989 and some minor changes have already been implemented. For example, solutions to heating and lighting problems have been found by the Medical Records Department team. The most significant findings of the teams are still being discussed - the ambulance service team is considering re-locating the authority's ambulance stations, and the main corridors team has suggested introducing retail shops into the hospital. The commercial viability of the shops is now being considered by the team.

Progress, however, has been generally slower than originally envisaged. As a result, each of the six teams that have been set up will now work more closely with their focus team mangers. It is intended that the managers will speed up the workings of the teams, and secure funding for any research they need to carry out. These managers have received training from consultants for this role.

TRADE UNION INVOLVEMENT

Pembrokeshire HA is not heavily unionised and has only around 50 per cent of its staff belonging to trade unions. There are, however, wide differences in membership across different sectors of the workforce. The ambulance service approaches 100 per cent trade union membership, while membership among ancillary workers, who are mostly part-time, is very low.

The Director of Personnel and Administration at Pembrokeshire HA, says that there has not been any trade union opposition to the quality improvement programmes. He believes that the 'Aspiring to Excellence' programme 'intrigued staff', particularly after the staff discontent following the efficiency and cost-cutting exercise carried out between 1982 and 1987. However, the authority is only in the early stages of promoting customer care and the staff are only beginning to adjust to this idea.

Effective customer care in the authority will be further enhanced by the introduction of a progressive management development programme which will be run in-house starting from September 1989. It is intended that the course will equip mangers with the knowledge, skills and attitudes to lead the development of excellence in patient care in Pembrokeshire HA in the 1990s.

PETERBOROUGH DISTRICT HEALTH AUTHORITY

Peterborough Health Authority forms the northwestern part of East Anglian Regional Health Authority, serving a population of 244,800. About 80 per cent of the authority's population live in and around Peterborough; the remainder of the authority consists mainly of rural fenland. The only other town of any size is the old market town of Stamford. Although Stamford lies outside its borders, Peterborough HA provides the town's hospital services.

Peterborough Health Authority employs around 3,000 staff (whole-time equivalents) in the following groups: nursing 52.7 per cent, medical 3.3 per cent, professional and technical 9.4 per cent, administrative and clerical 13.4 per cent, ancillaries 18.5 per cent, and building and maintenance staff 2.7 per cent. Most hospital services are provided by the authority except for specialities, like kidney dialysis, which are run by the regional health authority.

BACKGROUND

Peterborough HA has recently launched two major initiatives to improve the quality of the services it provides. During 1988, it established a Quality Assurance Department and introduced a number of customer care measures including quality circles and customer surveys. In July 1989, it launched an 'Employee Charter' in an effort to provide a positive and supportive work environment for its staff. This latter development is seen as essential by the authority if it is to succeed in its aim of providing an individual, sensitive and appropriate service to our customer'.

QUALITY CIRCLES

From April 1988, quality circles were set up in many areas of hospital activity. These include circles in the Catering and Works Departments, Medical Records, Outpatients and Wards. The circles are made up of staff volunteers from a wide selection of hospital jobs. The quality circle in the Elderly Unit, for example, consists of two nurses, one physiotherapist, a member of the catering staff, one porter and a person from medical records. The membership of the quality circle is completed by a 'facilitator' from the Quality Assurance Department. The chair of the quality circle is elected by its member. The authority stresses that although managers are often members of the quality circles in Peterborough HA, they are not management led.

Almost the only direction that quality circles receive from management is that the subjects discussed should have a customer or service orientation. However, on rare occasions, management may give a quality circle a specific problem to solve.

The usual procedure followed by quality circles is firstly to identify a problem, then to find its solution, and finally to present the solution to management. Since they were established, quality circles have found solutions to problems throughout Peterborough HA. The Estates Department quality circle recommended that a training video should be produced to educate staff on the dangers of putting unsuitable waste into the authority's waste-fuel boiler. The quality circle set up in Peterborough District Hospital Outpatients came up with four proposals designed to improve customer care: an overhaul of the complaints procedure, a 'who's who' board to make it easy for the public to identify staff, a patient information leaflet, and a patients' charter.

CUSTOMERS SURVEYS

In autumn 1988, following complaints from the public over staff attitudes and requests from the Community Health Council, Peterborough HA decided to review part of its hospital maternity service. As a first step, the Quality Assurance Department (QAD) interviewed a sample of women who had been discharged from maternity wards over the previous six months. The QAD passed on the information gathered from the interviews to the maternity ward staff at a special day-long meeting. Staff and the QAD then discussed the problems and came up with possible solutions which they communicated to senior management at the winding-up session. The evaluation of these proposals by management is still continuing.

TEAM BUILDING

The Quality Assurance Department has also been running 'team building' sessions in an attempt to raise the quality of service provided within the authority. Sessions have already been run in the Mental Health Unit, the Dietetic Unit and the Unit Management Team at the recently opened Edith Cavell Hospital. In the latter instance the QAD was brought in to help management make the transition from opening a new hospital to running it. With the help of the QAD, the Unit Management Team have clarified their individual roles within the team and reduced overlap, defined individual and team objectives, identified their training needs, and produced a plan of action.

THE EMPLOYEE CHARTER

In the autumn of 1988, the 'Personalised Service Group', a high level steering group, was set up to raise the profile of customer care in Peterborough HA and to push through further initiatives. However, it became clear at their early meetings, especially from feedback from quality circles, that a more caring managerial environment was a vital prerequisite for the successful development of customer care. The 'Personalised Service Group' therefore decided to concentrate initially on improving employee relations and staff working conditions. Only when these improvements had been made, reasoned the management, could they introduce effective customer care.

The result of these management deliberations was the 'Employee Charter', which was agreed in May 1989 by the trade unions and management and launched in the following July. The charter is intended to lay down clear guidance for managers to follow in their relations with staff. The provisions of the charter are varied but include the following demands on management. The managers in Peterborough HA will:

o   Treat every member of staff as an individual worthy of respect, courtesy and consideration;

o   Communicate freely and consult with staff on significant matters that affect them;

o   Provide, through Individual Performance Review, a clear statement of what is expected of each employee;

o   Attempt to provide fair and reasonable salaries equitably applied;

o   Provide a safe and pleasant work environment.

THE POSITIVE ACTION PROGRAMME

When they were formulating the Employee Charter, management was concerned that staff might take a cynical attitude if there was no action to back up the words of the charter. Management therefore introduced a 'Positive Action Programme', a 'major package of measures aimed at supporting staff and managers and encouraging excellence'. Management also ensured that a number of these measures were already in place in order to create staff confidence in the proposals. Among the more important measures were: the harmonisation of employment conditions, the introduction of equal opportunities policies, staff development, a review of communications, and health and welfare proposals.

Harmonisation Of Employment Conditions

This applies only to hospital ancillaries and removes some of the distinctions between weekly and monthly-paid staff. It includes the introduction of payment by credit transfer and the abolition of 'clocking' in and out of work.

Equal Opportunities

A number of initiatives have been launched as a result of joint management and staff representative meetings. These include: recruitment monitoring, a pilot survey of the workforce composition, training on assertiveness and a course on 'Women into management', new guidelines on harassment and extended leave, awareness training, and a holiday play scheme for the staffs' children.

Staff Development

The most important proposal is the extension of 'Individual Performance Review' (IPR) to all staff. In some health authorities it is only in use for managers receiving performance-related pay. Peterborough HA, however, believes that IPR will give all staff the opportunity to discuss work issues with management, improve communications between staff and management, and provide feedback from staff to management. Owing to the constraints of the national pay system there is no financial reward for staff who have performed well in their job. Instead, rewards will be in the form of increased job satisfaction, improved communication links with management, and better access to training.

The staff development proposals also include the introduction of a 'Development Award' of £3,000 to members of staff for the best training projects to improve patient care.

Communications Review

In September 1988, Peterborough HA sent a questionnaire to 10 per cent of its nursing staff on the issue of clinical regrading. The results of the questionnaire, as the authority expected, revealed problems of communication between staff and management. It appeared that communication and information about the regrading were worse at the lower levels of the nursing hierarchy. It also deteriorated further at every step down the hierarchy. As a consequence of this and other communication difficulties, a joint trade union and management study was set up in July 1989 in an attempt to improve consultation and communication in the health authority. One of its first tasks was to instigate a joint review of the formal mechanisms for consultation between management and the unions, the District Joint Staff Committee, and to improve its effectiveness.

Health And Welfare Proposals

In recognition of the high levels of stress in the NHS, a pilot scheme of staff counselling and support has been launched by Peterborough HA. Emphasis has been put on staff helping themselves, and to this end up to 300 staff are being trained this year in stress management. The authority hopes that this will help to build up support networks among staff. Additionally, more formal and advanced counselling training is being provided for 30 key staff. In the near future, the authority intends to produce a 'help booklet' for staff covering, for example, childcare, financial, housing and marital problems.

EMPLOYEE AND TRADE UNION RESPONSE

The response of staff to the customer care initiatives in Peterborough HA has been generally positive. The Employee Charter, however, was not enthusiastically received by union representatives on the District Joint Staff Committee. They felt that the charter did not contain sufficient concrete proposals to improve working conditions for staff.

Some elements of the Positive Action Programme, however, were received more favourably. In particular, the unions supported the introduction of payment by credit transfer and the establishment of a creche. The biggest trade union objection was to the extension of Individual Performance Review to all members of staff. In is NUPE national policy to oppose IPR.

THE COST OF CUSTOMER CARE

The cost of running the Quality Assurance Department is around £50,000 per annum, which pays for the three staff responsible and associated running costs. In 1988, the cost of hiring consultants added around £5,000 to the department's budget.

There was little cost, other than management time, in introducing the Employee Charter. But £14,000 has been put aside for implementing training programmes as part of the Positive Action Plan.

THE FUTURE

Management plans to carry out two staff attitude surveys to judge the impact of the Employment Charter six and then twelve months after its launch. Management hopes that the Employee Charter will help to create a working environment that is capable of promoting effective customer care.

Quality Assurance Department customer care initiatives continued while the Employee Charter was launched. However, from autumn 1989, health authority resources will be concentrated more fully towards customer care training. No detailed proposals have yet been finalised but the authority will attempt to 'incorporate customer care into the mainstream of managerial ability'.

TRENT REGIONAL HEALTH AUTHORITY

Trent Health Authority has the second highest population of any regional health authority in England. It is made up of twelve districts, covering the counties of Derbyshire, Leicestershire, Lincolnshire, Nottinghamshire and South Yorkshire. Trent Regional Health Authority employs around 1,500 people, most of whom are administrative and clerical staff, and runs region-wide functions such as the Blood Transfusion Service.

BACKGROUND

In 1985, Trent RHA was becoming increasingly concerned that it did not identify closely enough with the interests of customers. As a result it launched an initiative called 'Personalising the Service' that attempted to 'focus the attention of health service personnel on making service provision as sensitive 'as possible' to each individual patient or client'. Central to the Trent RHA initiative was the belief that patients must play a more active and participatory role in their treatment and care. Trent believes that a hospital should not be viewed as a large, impersonal organisation treating passive patients without regard to their views. In the case of the dying, for example, Trent RHA believes that there are social, as well as medical, models of care.

Increasing consumer sophistication was also an important motivation for Trent RHA to improve the care of its customers. Put simply, customers now expect a better standard of service. The private health sector, which has concentrated traditionally on providing high quality 'hotel services', has become more widespread and influential. The health service, however, is often criticised for the poor standards of its 'hotel services', which include the quality of food and the decoration and facilities of its waiting rooms. Finally, the centralisation of health services through the closing of the smaller, local hospitals in Trent RHA provided safer medical care, but this had been achieved at the expense of more personalised customer care.

PERSONALISING THE SERVICE

Trent RHA believed that the best way to achieve a personal service was by recognising good health service practice and publicising it. In January 1985, a working group was established with the aim of promoting a personal service within Trent RHA. The working group produced a document, 'Personalising the Service - The Trent Initiative, which took the form of a checklist for each district health authority to consider when formulating its personal service policies. The check list was divided into ten main headings: patient satisfaction, communication, element of choice, amenities, hotel

83

services, contact with the outside world, privacy, dignity and courtesy, confidentiality, counselling and bereavement.

The General Manager of Trent RHA was strongly involved in the initiative, using the story of Elsie Jones, an elderly patient who is beset by a succession of problems during her stay in hospital. The story illustrated the key features of what was meant by personal service. Most importantly, because staff recognised that they had met an 'Elsie Jones' in their jobs, it gained their support for the personal service initiative.

All twelve districts in the regional health authority actively supported the initiative, and in 1988 they were invited to display their successes at a regional exhibition on personal service. As a result, Trent RHA set up a personal services pilot project covering five units from four health districts. A management training resource package that uses a video, audio-cassette, and accompanying booklet entitled 'From Me To You', was produced as part of this regional pilot project to highlight the methods and achievements of the projects. The package is designed for use by managers who are planning to personalise their service. However, Trent RHA is keen to stress that a personal service 'can only be achieved by a partnership of management, staff and the consumer'. To promote this belief, a three coloured symbol of red, blue and green, signifying management, staff and the consumer respectively, was designed for the 'From Me To You' package.

THE NORTH DERBYSHIRE HA PILOT PROJECT

North Derbyshire, one of the pilot project districts, started its personal service project by focusing on its Accident and Emergency Department. The successes of this project are highlighted in the 'From Me To You' package. In 1986, a multi-disciplinary 'Patient Service Team', essentially a quality circle, was formed to develop ways of improving the quality of service to the consumer. The team was composed of six nursing staff, a radiographer, a receptionist, a porter, a domestic, a medical officer and a nurse tutor. The team, which met for one and a half hours each week, was given a time limit of six months (later extended to one year) to come up with proposals. Meetings were held in the form of workshops and run by a facilitator from the team. As the project progressed, other hospital staff were invited to the meetings to contribute their own views and knowledge. Visits were also made to other hospital units.

One of the more important decisions of the Patient Service Team was to commission a patients' questionnaire from the Consumer and Research Department within North Derbyshire Health Authority. The questionnaire was distributed to 193 patients (52 per cent of whom responded) attending the Accident and Emergency Department over a two week period. This revealed that over 90 per cent of patients were happy to return to the department, but that 82 per cent had visited the department without first contacting their GP. The questionnaire did, however, reveal dissatisfaction with the lack of information on waiting times and lack of facilities in the department. As a result, boards informing patients of waiting times are now displayed in the department. To counter the complaints about limited facilities, the department introduced music from the hospital radio, childrens' toys, magazines, fresh flowers and a television in the waiting room. The department has also produced information leaflets for the public and plans to redevelop the reception area and to appoint a nursery nurse.

Among the most important achievements of the Patient Service Team has been the establishment of the 'triage nursing system'. A triage or reception nurse, greets patients as they enter the department, and having assessed the seriousness of their condition, places them in an order of priority to be seen by a doctor. Since the introduction of the triage system, the number of complaints about long waiting times has fallen. Giving staff a say in the running of their department, and making them take responsibility for problems and their solutions, has led to the improved care of patients and increased staff satisfaction.

CARING FOR THE CARERS

In January 1989, Trent RHA launched Caring for the Carers, a regional pilot project. In common with the 'Personalising the Service' initiative, it offered to fund projects developed by districts and units within the regional health authority. This new initiative is only in its formative stages but progress has already been made. Counselling services, for example, have been set up for those who dealt with the casualties from the Hillsborough football ground disaster. Several health districts also operate a staff counselling service, which is run voluntarily by health visitors, occupational health staff and clinical psychologists. It now hopes to appoint a staff counsellor to publicise the merits of counselling and to evaluate and improve its effectiveness.

TRADE UNION AND EMPLOYEE RESPONSE

The trade unions in Trent RHA were consulted over all the 'Personalising the Service' initiatives. According to the Regional Personnel Manager, they were not opposed, but there was little positive response. He believes that the unions took this stance because they see an improvement in pay and conditions as the only real solutions to low morale in the health service.

Staff reaction to the initiatives has generally been mixed but more sceptical towards Caring for the Carers. They did not, for example, believe that it would help to solve management deficiencies. Staff attitudes to the more consumer care orientated measures, however, were different. The facilitator of the Patient Service Team in North Derbyshire HA commented that although staff were initially unwilling to cooperate with the team and its projects, they were prepared to become more involved when they saw that progress was being made.

THE PERSONNEL AND INDUSTRIAL RELATIONS IMPLICATIONS

In general, the personnel and industrial relations implications of the 'Personalising the Service' initiatives have been very limited. There have been no improvements to the pay and conditions of the majority of staff, although the performance related pay of the top managers was related to the success of 'From Me To You'. Benefits, however, have been realised in an increase in staff job satisfaction and an improvement in the quality of care patients receive. The Regional Personnel Manager and the Director of the Personal Service Initiative also claimed that working relationships between managers and staff, and also between professional and non-professional staff, have improved.

THE SUCCESS OF 'PERSONALISING THE SERVICE'

All districts and units in Trent RHA have been committed to improving the quality of the personal service to the customer. Personal service features in the various management review processes and is an important part of all planning decisions. The projects that became a part of 'From Me To You' have achieved most of their original aims. In addition to the North Derbyshire Accident and Emergency project, there were four other pilot projects:

o The North Lincolnshire Mental Health Unit which set out to develop a personal service for people suffering from mental illness.

o The 'People Our Priority' project at Pilgrim Hospital, South Lincolnshire.

o The Nottingham Community Unit which investigated what parents knew about and expected from the school health service.

o A project on the theme, 'First impressions on first contact with the hospital', from the University Hospital, Nottingham.

The Regional Personnel Manager believes that the 'Personalising the Service' initiative has created a more enjoyable and flexible working environment, and that this partially compensates for low pay. There are, however, staff shortages in the paramedical groups and also of some qualified nurses. This reflects low pay levels, competition for staff from the private sector and demographic change.

Trent is committed to continuing with the 'Personalising the Service' initiative, and during 1989 the lesson learned are being applied to the broader area of quality enhancement. A second regional exhibition, combined with three one-day conferences on personal services, clinical audit and 'Caring for the Carers', was held in September 1989 in Derby. It again used the practical experiences and enthusiasm of district and unit staff as a catalyst to stimulate further quality improvements.

The Cost Of Personalising The Service

The National Health Service Training Authority has provided financial support during the running of the regional pilot project to fund the resource package 'From Me To You. It has also funded the production of a nurse education package titled 'It Starts With Me' which looks at ways of applying personal service to nursing. Trent RHA also uses outside consultants when necessary and has created a regional post of Director for the Personal Service Initiative.

STROUD COLLEGE OF FURTHER EDUCATION

Stroud College serves a community of over 500 full-time and approximately 9,500 part-time and evening students, ranging from those taking two-year courses to those attending for one evening a week. Students are recruited from the South and East Gloucestershire area, and the college operates on a number of sites within the district.

The curriculum includes building technology, mechanical and production engineering, business studies, special education and general studies including several 'minority' A-level subjects and a variety of European languages. There is a School of Art in Stroud which holds courses on textiles, printing, pottery and photography as well as fine art. The 'standard student' at the college is a 16-19-year-old seeking A-levels or non-academic vocational training, but Stroud also serves a larger than normal part-time student body, including day release and adult education students.

The college employs over 100 full-time and 40 part-time teachers, along with approximately 60 support staff, such as technicians, secretaries, caretakers and refectory staff. Cleaning has been contracted out to the local authority DSO in the area.

BACKGROUND

Stroud college's 'mission statement' says that its aim is to 'serve the whole community'. The college defines of 'high-quality services' in terms of its ability to respond to community demands on the curriculum. Assessment of this demand is now increasingly market-led and the college has demonstrated its priorities by recently appointing a new Director of Marketing.

Two years ago, at the start of the 1987/88 session, the college was just beginning to emerge from a 'winter of discontent' in its recent history. A number of factors both inside and outside the college's control, in particular rapid turnover in the college Principal post, had conspired to create ineffective management, low staff morale, and a decline in enrolments. The first act of the current Principal, appointed in January 1988, was to review the structure of the college and set in train a process of revision, in consultation with staff, governors and the academic board. The new structure, now in its final stages of preparation, received a large vote in favour by staff.

The first phase of the new 'Marketing Further Education' policy, introduced by the Vice-Principal, increased enrolments over the two years by 30 per cent. This resulted in increased income for the college under the new Education Reform Act funding formula, and has placed the college in a position where it can effective begin to respond to the demands of the local community. This means putting into practice its customer care approach within the community. Stroud has already explicitly identified quality as the element which can distinctively differentiate its 'product' from that of other colleges, an approach effectively promoted by the college's new Director of Marketing.

THE MATRIX SYSTEM

The restructuring of the college's organisation on the basis of a modified 'matrix' system is seen as central to the provision of a flexible teaching programme responsive to customer needs. Under the new system, summarised in a report presented by the college Principal in mid-1988, the original departmental structure was broken down into a set of fourteen interacting course units. These are headed by 'line managers' at senior lecturer level, who report directly to the Vice Principal and Principal.

At senior management level, below the Principal and Vice Principal, is a Directorate of six people (graded as Heads of Departments), three of whom make up the Senior Review Team. It is their task to review and improve course provision. There are also Directors who co-ordinate college functions, such as Resources, the Curriculum, Adult and Continuing Education, Marketing, and Technology and Industrial Liaison.

The structure now consists of the Principal and Vice Principal, served by the Directorates and, beneath these, the twelve Line Managers responsible for courses within each unit of the curriculum. These units are grouped into three main categories - Services to Industry, Personal Services, and Services to Business - alongside the separate Special Programmes Unit which administers profit-making courses. Within these groups the courses range from motor vehicle and plant maintenance, through social studies and languages, to secretarial studies, business and management.

Organising courses within a unit-based matrix structure provides opportunities for flexibility and co-operation between subject areas which were precluded by the former departmental structure. Here, despite the large number of courses offered, different subject areas were 'hermetically sealed' from one another. While a student taking a technical course might also require, for example, business skills, it was extremely difficult under the previous system to span the two. Now, while every course is attached to a specific unit, they can all be serviced by teachers from different units. Further advantages of the new system are its breaking down of the previous hierarchical management structure and a reduction in the number of organisational levels.

Central to the effective operation of the matrix structure is the establishment of course teams, which may link one or more units through bringing together related subjects such as engineering, information technology and secretarial skills. The course teams are the target of quality monitoring within the college and are seen as an essential aspect of increasing flexibility and thus improving services. The course teams also provide input to the Central Curriculum Development Committee (CCDC), which is again seen as crucial to monitoring and improving the quality of college services. This consists of course unit or 'line' managers, who are advised by the course teams, along with the Senior Review Team. The committee meets monthly on a Friday afternoon which has been set aside from teaching for staff development, course team meetings and the CCDC.

COURSES AS COST CENTRES

The creation of this course unit matrix structure is partly aimed at making different courses much more independent. Some of the more commercial courses, catering directly to local industry, are expected to make a profit. This profit can be used to subsidise college resources via the mechanism of the Principal's development fund and to ensure better provision for disadvantaged students and the overall community. One unit manager, the head of the Special Programmes Unit, has no line management function but is responsible for administering these profit-generating courses, which include welding, word processing, languages, and computer-aided design and manufacturing (CAD/CAM).

All other units are expected to operate as cost centres and run their own budgets for materials and staff. The unit managers are required to monitor their expenditure against the amount allocated to them, based on their numbers of full-time students. Resources are provided to the college according to the county formula of approximately £2,300 per full-time student.

Within this system, it is impossible to 'hide' a superfluous member of staff, without the salary showing up as a negative input against overall expenditure. The budgeting process is also useful in providing information on how course units are operating. One result of the increased autonomy and market-led content of courses is a more flexible timetable. Where courses are tailored to the needs of the business community, the timetable can change from week to week. There can no longer be a 'year timetable' as in the past. This is most clear in the case of income-generating courses, but can also relate to basic training courses such as motor vehicle apprenticeships. Timetables must now adapt to business requirements rather than college needs. This is reflected in current national negotiations which are addressing the issue of 'averaging' of college hours (ensuring variable workloads are adjusted over the year).

The new system is seen by the Senior Review Team as 'getting the institution into better shape to respond to the demands of the marketplace'.

IMPROVING CUSTOMER SERVICES

Central to its market-based strategy is Stroud's adoption of a Quality Monitoring System, which draws most of its information from a set of questionnaires on student perceptions of colleges (EPOC). The college has been provided with funding from the government's Training Agency to assist it in fully introducing the system over the next two years.

This will require staff training in the use of the system, as well as the appointment of a full-time administrator and part-time secretary to implement the programme. These will be backed by a member of the academic staff whose task will be to ensure that the project is monitored and evaluated. This member of staff will be key in identifying staff development needs as part of the development of an overall quality management system based on the SPOC/EOPC information.

Open Learning Programme

Prior to the full implementation of SPOC/EPOC, the college has already introduced a number of schemes which can bring it in touch with the wider community. These include support for a programme of Open Learning (a community-based equivalent of the Open University in adult education). The county manager of Open Learning schemes is based in the college, and the college manages Open Learning premises in Stroud's town centre.

An access tutor is employed in order to reach a greater number of adults in the community, in addition to a specific tutor for the unemployed. The college runs a number of 'Drop-In' workshops in which members of the community can come and explore the range of courses offered, and a 'Drop-In Taster Week' has been run before the start of the college year. The college also backs a 'Work-Link' adult education scheme originally promoted by the Manpower Services Commission but now run independently by Stroud College.

Encouraging Returners

These initiatives have received an extra impetus through the drop in the number of 16 to 19 year old school leavers now entering the further education arena. The college now makes it a priority to encourage 'returnees' - unemployed and other adults who want to come back into full- or part-time education.

Part of this process is a strong emphasis on catering for the needs of disadvantaged students, such as those with disabilities or childcare problems. A creche is provided and the income generated from profit-making courses is used to provide facilities for the disabled. The aim of the college is to make itself 100 per cent accessible to disabled students, and this has been promoted through measures such as training reception staff to dealing with students who are hard of hearing. Braille boards for the blind are under consideration, and the college buildings have been converted to make them wheelchair-accessible wherever possible.

Helping Staff To Help The Customer

In addition to the major change towards a matrix structure, affecting mainly academic staff, the college is considering a number of measures to bring its support staff closer to a customer care perspective. These include consideration of a new employment structure, not yet implemented, in which secretarial, technical, maintenance and other support staff operate as functional teams rather than being tied to a specific department. This structure could include the possibility of incremental progression towards supervisory posts, and is seen as generally encouraging the growth of responsibility and autonomy for such workers.

The college is currently recruiting a Customer Care Officer to take charge of its reception area. This officer's task will be to encourage the development of a reception policy aimed specifically at creating a favourable initial impression for the customer. He or she will be one of a team of three in reception who will now report to the Marketing Director instead of to the Administrative Officer previously responsible for reception.

GETTING THE STRATEGY ACROSS

Training and improved communications for all levels of staff are important elements in getting Stroud's new market- and customer-led corporate strategy across to its workforce.

Training For Senior Staff

At senior academic staff level, training was given prior to the introduction of the new matrix course unit structure, through a residential course in which staff looked at how quality monitoring could be implemented in the college. Senior staff have also been through a training programme on the delegation of funding for courses, and further training will shortly be necessary for the implementation of the SPOC/EPOC programme.

Course unit or line managers are currently being trained in management techniques in order to prepare them for the relatively new task of running courses independently from any departmental structure. The type of training given includes all aspects of running a budget, along with inputs on marketing, quality and internal communications. This programme is run by a Staff Development Officer who works in collaboration with unit managers to find out what their training needs are, a process based on looking at existing management practice and how it is carried out. A weekly slot is set aside in the timetable for the workshop- and seminar-based training programme.

Training For Support Staff

Training on customer care has also been provided for support staff. In April 1989, two single days were set aside for support staff to consider the issue. They produced a report highlighting the main areas in which quality could be improved, specifically in providing clear information to students which could help them through the complexities of the college timetable.

PROMOTING THE CORPORATE CULTURE

A central feature of Stroud's new approach is the drive to impress on staff that the college now stands or falls on the quality of its services - delivery of courses, standards of care in reception, and so on. This comes down to the reality of jobs saved or lost - if Stroud does not succeed in attracting students, and is therefore 'funded under formula', it will have to reduce staff numbers. Jobs therefore depend on quality.

The college is putting this message across through a 'Bells and Whistles' pocket book on quality, issued to all staff, which emphasises the point that what makes Stroud different from other colleges is its high-quality services. The booklet is part of a major plan of staff development centred on a change in corporate culture in which it is accepted that concern for quality is essential to the survival of the college and is the responsibility of every employee. This new approach is now also symbolised in a changed corporate visual identity for the college, reflected in the design of letterheads, cards and college sweatshirts.

Communications Techniques

As part of putting across this change in perspective, some of the new teams set up (such as the Senior Review Team, the Senior Management Team, and the course teams) run their own Team Briefings process, which stems from the regular meetings held by these bodies to discuss quality, etc. Part of the function of all of these teams is to disseminate and share information.

Part of the remit of the new SPOC/EPOC programme is the improvement of quality not only through the key educational indicators provided by its survey but also in terms of non-educational factors, such as improved enrolment procedures, which involve non-teaching staff. The latter have themselves already pointed to the need for clearer college information for staff, and this has resulted in the proposal to publish a weekly 'programme of events' available to all staff.

EMPLOYEE RESPONSE TO THE STRATEGY

Most staff are now aware that this change in the corporate culture is what lies behind the recent major restructuring of college organisation. Aspects of this, such as the much greater flexibility and unpredictability of the course timetable, have caused resistance among some staff, while others have been able to adapt to the changes. In general, the requirement to budget for each course unit has, according to the college's marketing director, 'concentrated the minds' of staff who previously 'drifted along' without making a concerted effort to attract students. According to the new criteria, these units would now be overstaffed, and in many cases this has led to a rapid development of courses and the introduction of measures designed to improve their quality.

Unit managers are seen as responsible for the autonomous development of ideas within their own units, and have been told that the Principal 'doesn't want to see them unless things have gone completely off the rails'. If unit staff members see their unit manager's performance as unsatisfactory, there is a mechanism to remove the manager from leadership of the unit, although the replacement would not necessarily have Senior Lecturer status.

Given the college's emphasis on student needs and involvement, staff may feel excluded and an effort has therefore been made to extend maximum consultation to staff in introducing the new structures. Since course content and administration under the quality system is now highly client-centred, academic staff in particular may feel that their own views have now been excluded - a college lecturer is unlikely to have the same attitude towards a course as a sixteen-year-old student. This kind of professional input has therefore now been integrated into course preparation after the market research stage.

IMPACT ON STAFF

Despite all the efforts to involve and consult staff, the college says that some are still inflexible and unwilling to work to different timetables and year patterns. This is seen as a 'professional problem' rather than one relating to terms and conditions of service. However, some changes in pay and conditions are envisaged within the new structure. For example, profit sharing and profit incentives may be made available to staff in return for generating new courses. A new idea might win, for example, 25 per cent of the ensuing profits for the individual concerned.

The college is also discussing with NATFHE, the lecturers' union, the possibility of temporary upgrading of staff who have done the most to enhance the quality of a course over the academic year. The obstacle to this may be the agreement of acceptable measurements of quality.

The major changes likely to affect lecturers under the new consumer-oriented, market-led college programme will be in the areas of reduced class contact time, work load, and holiday and teaching periods. These are all being discussed and negotiated with the trade unions, which are themselves committed to a quality perspective. The internal negotiating structure has now been altered by the reorganisation, with one trade union representative drawn from each course unit.

COST IMPLICATIONS

The grant from the Training Agency for implementation of the SPOC/EPOC project is £63,000, half of which is taken up by start-up costs. The grant is scheduled to last two years, providing for running costs of the project of £20,000 per year, as well as extra staff costs. However, if only ten extra students are attracted to the college as a result of the project, this will mean increased income of £23,000.

Measures of success can be seen in terms of student numbers, but the criteria have to go further than this if 'quantity' is not to be substituted for 'quality'. Success in gaining qualifications, rates of course retakes and completions, and successful placing in employment, are some of the measures used in the SPOC/EPOC scheme. As yet Stroud is not in a position to measure its success precisely in these terms, but the new quality approach has already seen results in increased student numbers and a generally higher morale amongst both students and staff.

NORTHERN IRELAND DEPARTMENT OF ECONOMIC DEVELOPMENT

The Department of Economic Development carries out all the Northern Ireland functions of the Great Britain Department of Employment, the majority of those at the Department of Trade and Industry, and small parts that would come under the aegis of the Department of Social Security and the Department of Energy. The Industrial Development Board, which is an executive agency, also comes under its control. In addition, it is the sponsoring department for a number of public bodies, including the Fair Employment Agency, the Equal Opportunities Commission, the Northern Ireland Tourist Board and Enterprise Ulster. It employs around 3,000 people.

BACKGROUND

Much of the impetus to improve the Department's services has come from its Permanent Secretary, who has a strong personal commitment to customer care. The greatest barrier to improving quality in the department was judged to be its lack of central direction and clarity caused by the disparate nature of its operations. The department carries out a wide variety of functions and duties and it is also continually subjected to change. It was therefore decided that any policies introduced to improve the quality of service in the department needed to be flexible and adaptable.

In 1987, senior management were given the opportunity to set up task forces to break down the barriers between the often conflicting parts of the department, and to improve the quality of service provision. There were also task forces set up to foster competition, and to examine dependence on public sector financing. It was the Communications Task Force, however, that was established with a remit to improve service delivery to the people of Northern Ireland.

The need to improve the quality of service had been underlined by the results of a survey, carried out by consultants, on the attitudes of the public to the department. It also showed that the department had problems in effectively communicating its services to the public. The survey revealed, for example, that employers found the wide variety of employment services offered by the department very confusing and that, following from this, it was difficult to get consistent and cohesive advice. It was also found that while some services were popular (for example, the Youth Training Programme) the public did not necessarily associate these with the Department of Economic Development.

THE COMMUNICATIONS TASK FORCE

In order to address the problems raised by the survey, the Communications Task Force concentrated on improving the training of staff. The task force believed that, previously, training had been too low key in the department. One of its first actions was to appoint a training and development officer, but more importantly it started to push through customer care projects inspired by the book 'In Search of Excellence' by Peters and Waterman.

The Aims Of The Department

Following a succession of meetings between the Permanent Secretary and his under-secretaries, a document called the 'Aims Of The Department' was drawn up. It outlined three departmental aims:

o   The Economic Development Aim to strengthen the Northern Ireland economy by providing new employment and protecting existing jobs;

o   The Economic Service Aim to 'ensure that all the institutional and infrastructural services essential to the province's economic development are provided;

o   The Management Aim to demand efficiency and the transfer of resources from 'economic support to economic strengthening activities'.

Underpinning these aims is the belief that they can only be achieved if the staff are committed to achieving the 'highest standards of performance in all operations and dealings with their customers'.

The Value Statement

The next problem to be confronted was how to make the 'aims of the department meaningful, to the staff. The answer, which was a result of holding workshops for senior and middle management, was to draw up a 'Values Statement'. This statement effectively related the 'aims of the department' to every-day work by stressing specific values and principles that the staff should apply to their work.

In order to publicise these 'Values' a glossy publication was sent to all staff and a series of workshops organised in all the divisions of the department. The aim of the workshops was to involve all staff in examining the relevance of the 'Value Statement' to their jobs. It was hoped that they would apply it directly to their own work. For instance, the staff working in the Youth Training Division decided in their workshop that decentralising the division would be the most effective way of improving its service. This proposal is now under consideration by management. Management now faces the problem of trying to keep the momentum generated by the workshops going in the department.

THE SUCCESS OF THE COMMUNICATIONS TASK FORCE

According to the Assistant Secretary in the Personnel Division the success of the task force has been difficult to measure. This is partly because the original survey carried out to test the attitude of the public to the department was essentially anecdotal. It would not be possible to commission a follow-up survey that could accurately measure the progress made in improving the quality of the department's service. She believes, however, that there have been some identifiable achievements. Letters from customers, for example, are now usually answered according to a strict time-scale. Also, the department's telephone switchboard was improved following discussion at the workshops. There has also been discussion on how telephone calls should be answered. Many areas of the department have established standards of output and quality to be applied to the services they provide.

Team Briefing

Team briefings have been introduced throughout the department and are run on the Industrial Society model. Once every month key issues are pulled together as a 'core brief' by the Permanent Secretary. He communicates it down to his under-secretaries who then brief the assistant secretaries. It is their responsibility to pass the information on to all the staff in their divisions. This process, from the production of the brief to informing all the staff of it, must not exceed 48 hours. In an attempt to make the briefings as effective as possible, the assistant secretaries encourage staff questions and they also add information on local issues to the 'core brief'. These local issues are viewed as being more meaningful to junior staff because they relate directly to their own jobs.

Staff Appraisal

A new staff appraisal system has recently been introduced in the department. It is intended that the new system will not be wholly management led but will involve individual members of staff more fully in the appraisal process. Staff will draft their own job plans and then discuss them with management. Appropriate training will be made available to enable staff to contribute fully to the new appraisal system.

Employee Surveys

In June 1989, a survey and a report were completed on the opinions of 486 staff aged under 26 in the department. On the instruction of the Permanent Secretary, (in the belief that it would produce an honest and realistic report) the officers entrusted with this report were also under 26. This exercise demonstrates the department's attempt to encourage its staff to produce ideas and to follow them up with feasible proposals.

The Permanent Secretary also holds 'pathfinder lunches' every month to increase his contact with staff from the lower levels of the department. These are essentially straw-polls of staff opinion. A number of staff are invited to these lunches to a level just below that of office manager. Staff are encouraged to raise work issues that concern them and if necessary, the Permanent Secretary follows them up after the lunch.

Communications Branch

A new Communications Branch has been established and it has been responsible for initiating a number of new schemes. It has developed a corporate house-style, produced staff information bulletins and publications, and has also attempted to coordinate advertising throughout the Department of Economic Development.

TRADE UNION AND EMPLOYEE REACTION

The trade unions have not opposed any particular customer care measure introduced in the department but they were worried about the process as a whole. The Assistant Secretary in the Personnel Division believes that this is essentially because the quality improvement measures introduced involved all staff and not just trade union representatives. Union anxieties have since been overcome with management informing their representatives about any new initiatives. Furthermore, management has given the unions firm assurances that they will be consulted over any proposed changes arising from workshop discussions. Apart from 'isolated rumblings of cynicism' from staff that the quality improvement measures would do little for them, staff reaction has generally been positive. There has also been a greater tendency for junior staff to approach management with their ideas for improving the quality of the department's services.

The Personnel Division Assistant Secretary says that the customer care initiatives have created an 'atmosphere of excitement' in the department. The department has also become more 'action orientated' and not concerned solely with producing ideas. Managers more readily accept that mistakes will happen if progress towards improving the department's quality of service is to be made. The quality improvements in the department have been secured with only limited resources being made available. The Assistant Secretary believes that even more can be achieved in the future if these resources are increased.

BRITISH RAIL

British Rail is run as five businesses, - InterCity, Network South-East, Provincial, Freight and Parcels. These deliver the three major passenger services in addition to freight. While services are confined to Great Britain, increasingly the product on offer includes European and world-wide aspects.

British Rail employs 130,000 workers, of whom 25,000 are white-collar (management and clerical) and the rest workshop and engineering staff (40,000), traincrew (drivers and guards - 26,000), station and yard staff (17,000), supervisors (10,000), signalling staff (6,000) and miscellaneous (6,000).

Over the last few years staff numbers have been considerably reduced both through increased efficiency and the privatisation of various non-core activities such as shipping and hotels. Overall the traffic levels in the main business activities have been increasing.

BACKGROUND

In 1981 British Rail introduced a customer awareness initiative for its employees in face-to-face, daily contact with the public with the aim of improving staff behaviour towards these customers. However, this early attempt is now viewed as having been somewhat superficial, and the organisation is now concentrating on implanting quality management into the organisation rather than adopting merely the 'appearance' of customer care.

The new approach was signalled with the launch of a quality initiative early in 1988, but at that time no specific member of staff was made specifically responsible, as it was thought that the function could be carried out by a member of the British Rail Board. However, it was found to be impossible for any one member of the Board to divert sufficient time to the issue, and in 1989 a Director was appointed specifically for the 'Quality Through People' programme.

A 'Quality Network' has also been set up by the organisation with one representative from every region, function, business sector and staff department of British Rail. These representatives are termed Quality Managers or, in the smaller departments, Quality Leaders. A network of quality management has thus been created to cover the 22-24 segments of the organisation. This network links quality with value for money strategies so that individual departments become aware of where the organisation may be wasting money. It has also introduced some training initiatives, although these are separate from the major training programme shortly to be launched within the 'Quality Through People' project.

'Quality Through People' is presented as a major initiative aimed at changing the culture of the organisation. The programme is scheduled to take place over a period of three to four years and is aimed not only at improving services but also at tackling the low staff morale within the organisation.

There are many reasons why this initiative is seen as necessary. While British Rail has been increasingly successful in financial terms over the last few years, its services are still widely perceived as of low quality. The Director of 'Quality Through People', says that 'apparently we don't deliver what the customer wants'. This is seen partly as a result of having prioritised financial issues in the past. As a result, the organisation is now changing its focus towards quality.

An additional factor is competition. British Rail has only a small share of the transport market, and this market is becoming increasingly competitive. As the Quality Director sees it, 'people expect more and better'. However, he makes clear that the quality initiative is not a response to privatisation rumours.

Finally, an important factor is the attitude of staff. The results of an internal report in 1988 are described as 'quite frightening', with 'total disaffection' in some areas and a 'lack of identity with British Rail Board objectives'. The Director of 'Quality Through People' emphasises that BR has a committed workforce. However, in his view that commitment could be put to better effect by management and staff working in the same direction. However, it was made clear in the report that staff see British Rail as a service rather than a business, and while the Board thinks it can be both , staff are convinced that the objectives are contradictory.

RESTRUCTURING FOR CHANGE

In the competitive atmosphere of the last few years, British Rail has moved increasingly towards selling off all aspects of the business not directly connected with the 'core railway' business. Examples have been the Sealink ferries, the hotels, Hoverspeed, British Transport Advertising, British Rail Engineering Limited (BREL) and Travellers' Fare, the station catering arm. As part of this process, many support services, such as cleaning, security and building maintenance, have been put out to tender.

In 1982 the business was reorganised on the basis of 'sector management' with an increasing bias towards decentralisation. This led to the creation of five separate businesses with targets set by the Board. Within this structure British Rail has now established a series of self-accounting units on a contractor-client basis. These services are set up as independent units which in due course will be able to trade both with BR and with other organisations.

COMMUNICATING THE STRATEGY

'Quality Through People' is seen as being about fundamental cultural change within the organisation, rather than imparting superficial quality 'techniques'. The training strategy to be undertaken within the programme begins with issues of attitudes and behaviour. It is being carried out on a 'cascade' basis, beginning with a programme called 'Leadership 500' for the top management within the organisation. This centres on the culture of the organisation and management attitudes towards quality and leadership.

Training for the 'Leadership 500' has consisted of a week-long course at a residential college, in which leadership and quality issues were debated. The top managers were grouped into syndicates of six, of which at least five were cross-functional in their working relationships. Outside consultants were used at this level, with groups being asked to produce a 'vision' of what their service could become and to then see it as their responsibility to put this into practice.

The next level of the 'cascade', taking in the next tier of senior managers, is about to begin on a pilot basis. This will involve a greater emphasis on quality standards themselves, and more local content. The cascade process is timed to take in all 130,000 employees within the organisation over the next three years. The next level will be the 8,000 middle managers and senior supervisors. As the training 'cascades' down through the organisation, it will be carried out in 'different but appropriate' ways, with more localised application.

Some more short-term training on quality skills has also recently been carried out within the organisation. This has included training in teamwork and quality skills, and also some instruction on the application of quality standard BS5750. The training has been carried out through a small number of separate weekly courses, arranged on a modular basis.

EMPLOYEE RESPONSE

It is hoped that the currently negative attitude among staff towards BR's moves towards quality will be changed through the application of the training programme. At present, many employees see management's agenda as about saving money, rather than delivering quality.

However, this disaffection is contradicted by an extremely high level of commitment to the industry itself, says BR. If management can demonstrate that it is sincere in wanting a good service, this may overcome the view of many employees that managers do not care about their staff or the industry and are only interested in what the 'bottom line' (minimum profit margin) looks like. Much of the cynicism is found at the lowest grades within the organisation, and it is hoped that the 'Quality Through People' initiative will ensure that a quality perspective does not come as a complete culture shock to the 90,000 staff in the lowest grades. By the time that the programme reaches this level in 1991, it is hoped that staff will have seen their managers and supervisors operating in a different way and may therefore be persuaded that management is serious in seeking a genuine improvement in quality within the organisation.

Communication And Awareness

At present, however, the 'Quality Through People' programme is at a very early stage. The directorate is concentrating on maximising the awareness of senior management through producing a number of training publications including an 'orientation package'. A monthly newsletter has also now been launched, which goes only to people who have attended the programmes. This is used to keep them in touch with what is happening as the project develops.

BR is also spreading its new quality approach to employees through its monthly newspaper, Rail News, and is putting out management briefs and press releases on this topic fairly regularly.

Other methods of communication have included team briefings, for example in Parcels, but these have met with a mixed response and 'not a lot of feedback'. The Staff Suggestion Scheme was relaunched in 1988 and is now said to be much more successful. It now has its own manager and offers a wide range of awards. The employee survey carried out in September 1988 was the first such survey at British Rail but there are now plans to repeat it at regular intervals.

More Flexible Working Patterns

In a large nationalised industry such as British Rail, with centrally-negotiated agreements, any moves towards linking pay and working patterns to service quality may seem a long way off. However, some of the initiatives taken in restructuring British Rail as a business have made a clear link between the terms and conditions offered to staff and the content of service delivery. Increasingly, individual parts of the industry are developing hours and payment packages on a more flexible basis than the traditional 40-hour week.

British Rail's proposed new bargaining arrangements are designed to take this approach further through adopting a functional/operational basis for negotiations. For example areas like engineering (divided into civil engineering, mechanical and signals) will become an independent bargaining unit. BR says, that this proposal is aimed at making pay and conditions more relevant to particular occupational groups, rather than the existing generic 'BR employees'. However, these moves have not been proposed as part of a specific initiative to improve service quality, but mainly because the bargaining structure, originally introduced in 1956 for a workforce of 500,000, is now seen by management as seriously out of date.

The various internal businesses now function on an entirely new basis. Red Star, for example, despite being a major business in its own right, has to operate on the margin of British Rail's other activities and stand alone. As part of this process a pay and staffing package which is relevant to the parcels market, and not to railways, is seen as necessary by management.

Trade Union Response

The new approach to quality has been discussed with BR's trade unions through the British Rail Council, a national consultative body. According to the 'Quality Through People' director, there was a reaction but many union representatives felt they had 'seen it all before'. The unions were also invited to attend the Leadership 500 stage of the quality training programme.

The job of the quality directorate will be to convince the unions that they are serious and that they are now addressing a much broader range of issues. This is seen as much more likely now that the commitment of the Chairman and top management of British Rail has been given to the 'Quality Through People' initiative.

THE FUTURE

The 'Quality Through People' initiative is seen by BR as a fundamental cultural change within the organisation. The promotion of a set of core values within the organisation is seen as essential, and this is currently a part of the work of the 'Quality Through People' directorate. Its 'core values' have not yet been published, but a Vision Statement has now been drawn up which has received the Board's blessing. British Rail already has a strong corporate identity, but this has until now not been expressed as a statement of the organisation's values.

It is too early in the process for British Rail to be able to measure the success of its quality initiatives, but a substantial investment in the project has been made by the Board. No limits have been attached to the budget for the project. In general, the process is not measured by the management in terms of cost but in terms of meeting long-delayed quality targets. As such, it is seen as an 'act of faith', but, according to the 'Quality Through People' director, there is no reason why the initiative should not achieve both substantial quality improvement and significant reductions in cost.

ROYAL MAIL LETTERS - GLASGOW DISTRICT

The Glasgow District of Royal Mail Letters covers around 5,500 square miles of central and west Scotland, including the west coast islands. The larger towns in the region are Glasgow, Paisley, Motherwell, Ayr, Kilmarnock, Dumbarton and Oban. The population of this area is around three million.

On 1 October 1986, the Post office was divided into four parts: Counters, Parcels, Letters and Giro Bank. The letters division in Glasgow offers the following services: Mailsort, Business Reply, Freepost, PO Boxes, Domestic Mail, Letter Contracts and Direct Mail. To run these services 5,600 people are employed by the district. Out of a total of around 52 million letters posted each day in the UK, over 6 million letters pass through the Glasgow sorting office.

BACKGROUND

In 1984 a 'Code Of Practice' was launched by the Post Office to explain to its customers the quality of service they should expect to receive. Following a favourable reaction from the public to the document, a national customer care programme was introduced by the Post Office in 1987. Pressure to improve the quality of service had also come from the Post Office Users National Council.

Specialist Customer Care departments were set up in Post Office districts following the reorganisation of the Post Office in October 1986. There was already a 'Correspondence Branch' in Glasgow, which dealt with enquiries and complaints, but this department did not deal with enquiries in these areas alone and had only eight staff. With the establishment of the 'Customer Care Unit' these staff, all of whom joined the new unit, were increased in number to 25 and they now work solely on customer care issues.

A 'Business Customer Care Unit' with six staff was established in 1988 to fulfil similar functions for the Post Office's business customers. The importance of maintaining good links with the business community is recognised by the Post Office, especially because of the possibility of the Post Office's letter monopoly being taken away. In addition to its customer care obligations, staff also have a sales role, being responsible for increasing the level of business post. A further 25 staff deal with undeliverable items of mail and handle postcode enquiries.

National And Local Training Initiatives

In 1987, the first national initiative towards promoting customer care was launched with the introduction of two and a half day training courses in Bedford for clerical staff. All clerical staff attended a 'job skills' course and new staff went on a 'job knowledge' course. The latter provided an introduction to Post Office services and concentrated on the methods of dealing with complaints and enquiries. The 'job skills' course covered similar ground but in more depth.

Following the setting up of Business Customer Care in 1988, the Post Office introduced 'Masterclass', a national mail room training scheme for big business users of the Post Office. The service, which costs a nominal sum of £50 per day, is designed to train mail room supervisors to organise their letters properly before Post Office collection. This training service not only assists the Post Office in sorting and classifying business mail, but is also seen as engendering business confidence in the Post Office. Before this national scheme was introduced, Glasgow had carried out a less advanced, but free, training service that was more geared to the mail room junior. It is planned that this service will continue.

'Cycle Training', a new national initiative, has also been introduced. It is designed to inform all staff, through meetings held every month, of new services or changes to existing services.

In addition to these national initiatives there has also been a large amount of local training carried out in Glasgow. Customer Care Unit staff were sent on a two-day Industrial Society course in 1987 to introduce them to the concept of the 'customer'. Training provision has also been extended to office delivery staff. They have received on-the-job training from their office managers with the help of various training aids and booklets. There have also been efforts to get Customer Care Unit and office delivery staff to visit each other so that they can appreciate each other's problems. In January and February 1988, for example, all Customer Care Unit staff went on street delivery rounds.

DEALING WITH COMPLAINTS AND ENQUIRIES

In 1987 the Post Office introduced a national scheme in order to standardise the procedures for dealing with complaints and enquiries from the public. Most importantly, the procedures laid down maximum time limits for the Post Office to answer three types of enquiry. Work is graded as 'rapid', 'action' or 'planned', depending on the time allowed to answer the enquiry. If, for example, a single letter has gone astray, the Post Office must provide a 'rapid' response and answer the complaint within five working days. A complaint about, for example, general delays to postal deliveries in a specific area, is classed as 'action' and a reply is required within three weeks. This more generous time limit would allow the Post Office, in this example, to conduct tests on the postal route. Finally, for a more serious complaint, for example the loss of a registered letter, the Post Office is required to make a 'planned' response which can take up to six weeks. In all these cases, complaints are acknowledged through sending a letter to the customer. In the latter case, an interim letter reporting on progress is sent to the customer after two weeks. Computers are used to keep detailed records of all complaints.

Effective monitoring of the performance of the Post Office districts is achieved through the results of short questionnaires sent to customers who have made an enquiry or complaint to the Post Office. A national scheme has been set up to reward the customer care units that meet the enquiry targets and provide a good service. The Glasgow Customer Care Unit has already received five national awards.

In Glasgow itself, a local incentive scheme is run to further reward good performance. All sections are requested to take responsibility for customer care in their own departments and platinum, gold, silver, and bronze awards can be given. Awards include a free hair-cut or £10, a free lunch and a free dinner.

IMPROVING COMMUNICATIONS

The Glasgow Customer Care Unit is also determined to improve the communication links between itself and the delivery offices throughout the district. The Unit now provides a list of 'failures' every month to the delivery office manager and this is then passed on to the staff. This close communication allows the delivery office to quickly identify and rectify the causes of the complaint. For example, if complaints reach the Customer Care Unit that a delivery in an area is persistently late (9.30am should be the latest time for a morning delivery), effective communication links with the relevant delivery office could lead to the solution of the problem through the swift implementation of revised workloads.

The Business Customer Care Unit sees its role in dealing with complaints as more positive. Since its inception the unit has been attempting to form close links with business so that its response is quicker when complaints arise.

TEAM BRIEFINGS

Team briefings are another new development which have been introduced nationally by the Post Office to improve the quality of services. These are run on the basis of the Industrial Society model, which suggests that the content of the briefings might include the four 'P's':

o   Progress - This might include the department's performance against target or budget and the success or failure of projects.

o   Policy - Changes in, for example, systems, routines, or staffing arrangements.

107

o   People - This could include promotions, transfers, new arrivals.

o   Points for action - This could include quality, safety, special jobs.

Team briefings are held once every month for all staff and are divided into two parts. The 'core brief', which is written by the relevant line manager and generally covers policy matters, is followed by a briefing by the departmental manager to staff on more 'day-to-day' matters.

TRADE UNION RESPONSE

The Union of Communication Workers' response to the team briefings is to encourage 'passive participation' or, in other words, for staff to listen to management briefings but not to discuss the issues raised. This policy is a result of union reaction to attempts by management at team briefings in some districts to persuade staff to vote against industrial action in 1988. In Glasgow this trade union opposition has caused some problems in team briefings held in operational units.

With the exception of the opposition to team briefings, the unions have been very much behind attempts to improve services. There is a national 'blueprint' for the development of customer care but there is a large amount of local discretion allowed in deciding how to implement it. Negotiations with the unions at local level were undertaken when the 'blueprint' was established nationally.

According to the Glasgow District Personnel and Industrial Relations Manager, the employees welcomed changes brought about by the introduction of customer care because 'they were made to feel part of them'. For example, all the staff discussed how to respond to telephone callers and decided that all telephones should be allowed to ring a maximum of three times before being answered. In the national blueprint a maximum of five rings is allowed.

Changes in the pay and conditions of Post Office staff have played little role in improving customer care and quality improvement programmes. There is, however, an individual bonus scheme for managers earning £11,500 and above per annum. This can be paid to a maximum of one and a half per cent of the paybill and is based on an annual performance appraisal.

SUCCESS OF CUSTOMER CARE

Since October 1986, when the Glasgow district of Royal Mail Letters was established, a higher proportion of letters are being delivered on time. The rate of first class letters delivered the following day has risen by two to three per cent and the success rate for second class letters by over 10 per cent. The Personnel and Industrial Relations Manager believes that part of this improvement in the quality of service is attributable to the district's customer care strategy.

He also believes that Customer Care has been very beneficial by increasing staff morale and job satisfaction. It has also engendered a more responsible attitude among staff to work and this has obviously improved the quality of service to customers. Staff in the Business Customer Care Unit, for example, are organised to cover different areas of the district and individuals in the Unit therefore become well known to the customer and are able to offer a more personalised service.

A continuous improvement in customer care is one of the major aims of Royal Mail. In Glasgow this includes introducing computers to deal with postcode enquiries, rationalising collection and delivery arrangements, and increasing staff training. It also includes full consideration being given to new services, such as Sunday collections.

BRITISH AIRWAYS

British Airways, which was privatised in 1987, expanded to merge with British Caledonian in 1988 and during that year carried almost 25 million people on its scheduled and charter services. The company employs approximately 49,000 staff, 44,100 in the UK and the rest abroad.

BACKGROUND

The early 1980s saw a significant downturn in the air transport industry in which a number of airlines faced bankruptcy. British Airways reacted to this downturn with a 'Survival Plan' which included the following features:

o   A significant reduction in staff by approximately one third, from 58,000 to 38,000.

o   A streamlining of the operation, including elimination of less profitable routes.

o   A reconfiguration of the fleet in which the less cost-effective aircraft, such as the VC10s and Boeing 707s, were sold off.

The reduction in staff numbers, which was achieved by voluntary severance and redeployment, necessitated a considerable increase in productivity. This was made possible by the removal of demarcation and other restrictive practices. The co-operation of staff and trade unions was essential, and this was achieved through the British Airways Trade Union Council (BATUC), a body specifically set up to consult with the unions over BA's Survival Plan separately from any pay and conditions issues.

The result of the survival exercise was, by 1983, a turnaround in British Airways' fortunes from a loss-making organisation to one which was both in profit and in a very strong position to forge ahead in world competition and growth. Now that the company was both financially and technically viable, therefore, the next step was to consider those factors which would put it ahead of the competition. The principal factor was seen to be customer care.

CUSTOMER INITIATIVES

A number of initiatives were therefore launched at this time to improve BA's service to the customer. The first of these was the ordering of a number of new aircraft, along with new uniforms for staff featuring BA's changed logo. These were given a high-publicity launch which highlighted the company's change of perspective in the direction of the customer.

At the same time the company was reorganised in order to shift its focus from the traditional emphasis on technology towards marketing and customer care. Safety has always been regarded as paramount and this will continue to be the case.

The reorganisation was launched on the basis of an extensive survey of British Airways customers carried out in 1983. This showed that while BA was perceived as highly efficient and technically competent, its staff were seen as lacking in a caring and personalised approach. The decision was therefore taken by BA's Chief Executive that priority must be given to changing this perception and maximising the organisation's concern for the customer.

RESTRUCTURING FOR CHANGE

The company is now establishing its regional bases, (for example Birmingham, Manchester and Scotland), as independent Strategic Business Units which are expected to be self-financing. Within the central organisation itself, departments are now required increasingly to pay for internal services and charge for their own services. The aim is to make each department responsible for its own budget rather than depending on central resources.

Along with this has gone an increasing decentralisation of departmental functions. The Human Resources function, for example, has now been devolved to line management, with the Human Resources Department itself slimmed to a core of staff who act as consultants to these managers. The aim is not only to save money through reducing the size of the department but also to enable line managers to build up a greater rapport with their staff which will be reflected in better care for the customer.

In general, departments are now encouraged to recognise that 'we all have customers' - internal departments being as important to those who serve them as the external customers are to 'front-line' staff.

IMPLEMENTING THE STRATEGY

British Airways' 'Customer First' programme of training for all staff began with the two-day course, 'Putting People First' (PPF). This was designed to help each individual employee recognise how he or she responds to treatment from other people, and thus to make them more aware of the customer. The course was provided initially for those staff with direct customer contact and was then extended to cover all staff within the organisation. It took place in the company training centre.

'Putting People First 2' followed. Here the initial PPF approach was simply adapted to provide training directly related to the activities of individual departments and the people working in them. To back up the training received in the PPF2 package, employees have been organised into customer care teams, similar to quality circles, in which staff and supervision meet to talk about problems and jointly identify ways in which they can improve services.

The next phase of training, 'A Day in the Life', was designed to meet a need identified by staff themselves. Staff felt that they needed a better understanding of the way other departments functioned within the airline. Again, this programme was aimed at all staff, not just those in contact with the public. Employees were invited to demonstrations run by other employees (after prior training), in which they presented the work of their department. This was a one-day course, held in the company's training centre.

'TO BE THE BEST'

The most recent training course, 'To be the Best', was a one-day programme, focussed specifically on the airline's competitive position. This gave staff the opportunity to watch videos on the business practices of other major carriers. They were then encouraged to make suggestions on how to compete more effectively; all these suggestions were considered. This course has now been completed and work is in hand on developing a new course.

In order to back up the customer care training and ensure that these programmes are extended to all staff in a workforce which is necessarily mobile, the company has recently linked up with the Open Learning Programme, (in this case based at the Central Manchester College of Technology) to provide distance learning on customer care for its cabin staff. The open learning system is flexible enough for the student to organise his or her own study programme to fit around the variability of the work patterns. About 150 stewards and stewardesses are now on the course, which offers a diverse syllabus including self-presentation, managing difficult situations and cultural awareness of other societies.

Management Courses

One objective within the overall training exercise was that of retraining British Airways management. All managers have now been put through a residential week of education and training entitled 'Managing People First' (MPF). This course is designed to enhance managerial techniques and self-awareness, as well as improving relationships between staff and their customers. Staff care within British Airways is seen as an essential component of customer care.

'Managing People First' encourages managers to develop awareness of motivation, trust and vision. They are then asked to produce a mission statement for themselves and for the group, on the basis of which they can shape their own future activities.

The course is organised on a cross-departmental basis, bringing together a group of about 25 managers. This group is then broken up into smaller groups, under a dedicated course tutor. In addition to the human resources skills taught on the course, there is the opportunity to build networks with other staff, which in an organisation as large as BA can often be difficult. Groups which have been formed on the course are encouraged to meet afterwards from time to time.

MPF has been followed by 'Leading the Service Business', a further management course where the focus is on competition. Finally, the company's induction course, 'Welcome to British Airways', contains a strong customer care component. This was originally a two-day programme but has now been refined down to one day. It was first launched in 1987 after privatisation; before that time the company had not run a formal induction programme for new employees.

Performance Management and 'Key Results'

A central aspect of the management training programme, particularly 'Managing People First', is its integration with the Performance Management System. This, a form of managerial performance appraisal and development linked to performance-related pay, focuses on the twin criteria of 'Key Results Areas' and 'Management Behaviours'. The 'Managing People First' training programme sets the basis for the system by providing subordinate and peer appraisal of each manager's behaviour against a list of agreed characteristics. The behavioural criteria are then monitored and assessed, in conjunction with the assessment of achievement of 'Key Results Areas', as the basis for performance-related pay and for personal development plans.

EMPLOYEES RESPONSE

The British Airways Trade Union Council, central to the success of BA's original 'Survival Plan', was also involved in the establishment of a number of 'joint participative studies', in which staff in specific areas (Highlands and Islands was an early example) were involved in setting and achieving targets for the business. Part of this process was 'opening the books' to the staff, who then came up with a number of 'quite dramatic' changes in the way operations were run.

These moves have set a pattern of extensive staff and trade union involvement in change, which is now heightened by a successful profit-sharing scheme for all employees launched with privatisation. The scheme has been promoted as part of the customer care approach on the basis that improved services to customers will mean higher profits. At the end of the 1988-9 financial year this scheme paid out three and a half weeks' salary to the workforce - in fact the bonus was equivalent to two and a half weeks' pay, but the company decided to add on an extra week in tribute to the 'first-class job' employees were said to have done during the year.

In addition, the company operates a Savings Related Share Option scheme for its staff, which has achieved a high degree of take-up - 40 per cent of staff have opted to join, as opposed to the norm in other organisations of 16-25 per cent. The average amount saved by those participating in the scheme is approximately £50 per month, again higher than the average of roughly half this figure.

These schemes have both acted to increase employees' sense of involvement with the company and to foster a positive attitude towards and interest in maintaining the airline's customer care reputation. A further scheme which has promoted this sense of involvement is 'Brainwaves', a high-profile suggestion scheme offering rewards of up to £10,000 for some suggestions. Awards totalling more than £92,000 were shared by 476 staff during 1988-9 under the scheme, which was launched in 1983-4 but recently revamped with extra publicity.

Communications with the Workforce

Other forms of communication between management and workforce are well developed. Regular Team Briefings are held, although the frequency of meetings depends on individual managers within the departments. Any major piece of information, such as the purchase of new aircraft, is directly communicated to the workforce through a specific Briefing Note circulated to all staff.

The management is proud of its weekly staff newspaper, British Airways News, which in addition to the unusual frequency of its publication (most staff newspapers are monthly) is said to be of particularly high quality and has won a number of awards. The newspaper incorporates a letters page which provides a forum for staff to communicate their views.

In addition, videos are produced every quarter in order to inform staff about the company's financial results. A VideoPoint system, with display units at selected terminals, has now been piloted with some staff groups - this provides staff with an opportunity to raise questions, the answers to which are incorporated within the video.

To add to the level of employee response, staff are invited to fill in assessment forms on training when they complete their courses. The comments made are then incorporated into the reformulation of these courses. They also have an opportunity of putting questions, and expressing points of view, to the Chief Executive or other Senior Directors at an open forum at some point during each course.

The positive nature of employee response to the training programmes and overall customer care initiative is said to 'speak for itself' in the generally high level of customer service now provided by the company. Most employees now 'recognise the significance of the customer' and customer response, monitored in a number of surveys carried out since privatisation, reflects this change.

PUTTING ACROSS THE CORPORATE CULTURE

Like many other organisations setting out to make customer care a priority, British Airways is anxious to achieve a corporate culture across the company centred on this goal. The changed logo, uniforms and aircraft design introduced with privatisation are seen as symbolising this corporate identity, one which has been widely accepted by the workforce. The company's values are spelt out in the Chief Executive's Mission Statement, which is printed on a small plastic card issued to every employee either at induction or on completion of a training course. This corporate culture is also put across through a number of promotional activities within the company such as 'Awards For Excellence' which recognise and reward particular contributions in delivering customer care in the course of the individual's job.

An additional initiative has recently been introduced in the form of relaunches of the company's separate services, such as Club World and Club Europe, First Class, and now Super Shuttle to be followed by Economy in the near future. These relaunches have involved extensive surveys on customer requirements, resulting for example in the introduction of personalised videos and luxury glass and china into the First Class service. In the years since improvements were made in the airline's Club World and Club Europe business services, traffic in these classes has increased appreciably.

COST IMPLICATIONS AND MEASURES OF SUCCESS

British Airways' training programmes on customer care have involved the company in a substantial financial commitment - the induction course alone is estimated to cost £35 a day per person, excluding salary and travelling expenses - but this is seen as entirely necessary in terms of supporting a core business activity. The investment in training has been more than recouped in business returns; the Annual Report for 1988-9 shows almost a doubling in turnover over the last four or five years from £2,943m in 1984-5 to £4,257m in 1988-9. The considerable investment put into training and other customer care initiatives is seen as wholly justified in this context.

British Airways' success in improving its competitive position through a customer-oriented, high-quality approach has been spectacularly endorsed by the number of world-class awards received by the company since completion of its 'Survival Plan'. The airline is now judged as first in world terms on a wide range of aspects of customer service.

BRITISH TELECOM

British Telecom, privatised in 1984, employs 232,000 people in its three main divisions, -British Telecom UK (which has 29 districts), Communications Systems, and British Telecom International. Subsidiary companies employ a further 12,400.

BACKGROUND

British Telecom is committed to a policy of 'Total Quality Management' (TQM). This is made clear in its Annual Report for 1989, which states: 'We are committed to far-reaching changes in our culture through Total Quality Management to enable us to meet customers' requirements first time, every time, as part of our normal business activity'.

This policy was initiated in 1986, when it covered only one part (UK Operations) of the business. The policy has now been integrated into every part of the company, including its subsidiaries.

There are three main driving forces behind this development:

o **Competition** The company was privatised in 1984, and since then has competed with a number of other companies offering similar services. Aiming for quality is seen as a way of remaining competitive - the company must provide high quality services to survive.

o **Reducing Failure Costs** Getting products and services 'right first time' cuts down on the costs of the checking process, as well as the cost of putting right things that have gone wrong.

o **Culture** This is seen as 'the most fundamental reason' behind the introduction of the Total Quality Management programme. The major changes which have taken place within BT, from its origins as a Civil Service department to its eventual status as a nationalised industry, and then to privatisation, have required significant changes to some deeply-entrenched employee attitudes. However, BT says that much of its culture is still rooted in its past. The new quality programme is seen as providing the opportunity to make a 'quantum leap' away from this earlier culture.

Part of BT's past tradition was a management system based on written instructions from the top. Within the TQM framework, a system of team-based organisational structures is being created, which is aimed at the development of responsibility and devolution of authority throughout the organisation. Where previously there was a failure to listen, the organisation now encourages a high degree of feedback from its employees. Participation and informality are central aspects of this shift in the organisational culture.

RESTRUCTURING FOR CHANGE

While not directly co-ordinated with the TQM programme, there have recently been significant organisational changes within BT. The three major businesses, BT/UK, International, and Communications Systems, were until recently operated as independent profit centres. A matrix/team approach is now being introduced across the Group which defines the relationships and inter-dependencies of these three major business areas. This approach, which starts at the highest level of management, is helping to break down departmental barriers.

WORKING FOR TOTAL QUALITY

Quality Improvement Projects first began in 1986, with the launching of TQM, and are still seen as the best way of developing teamwork within the organisation. The quality improvement programme set out to do two things:

o   To achieve a substantial increase in the rate and effectiveness of problem-solving.

o   To provide practical opportunities for practising teamwork and other aspects of the change in culture.

Multi-disciplinary teams were set up which brought together employees from different departments in a structure which set aside the usual heirarchies, for example staff in engineering, sales and accounting. More than 2,000 teams are now in existence and a great variety of quality improvement issues are being examined. 200 Quality Improvement Projects have already been completed.

These teams are monitored by over 50 'Quality Councils' made up of senior managers within business units. These managers approve, set and monitor the quality criteria for team projects on the basis of the 'Crosby five-stage project approach', ie:

1.   Define the problem
2.   Problem Analysis and Planning
3.   Action Plan
4.   Implementation Plans
5.   Implementation

TRAINING STRATEGY

Clearly a quality improvement programme on this scale requires a considerable training input. Training within the organisation has been centred around general workshops and specific training in problem-solving techniques, such as 'brainstorming', or 'Pareto Analysis'. While BT had initial help from consultants in setting up these training arrangements, they are now almost entirely specified and run 'in-house', including production of all training documentation and materials.

Overall training on quality within the organisation can be divided into three stages:

o **Initial Awareness Training,** taking up half or a whole working day, in which standard packages, incorporating videos, slide shows and discussions sessions, are presented within all units. All staff have now been through this programme, which took place during the first two years of Total Quality Management.

o **Three-day Workshop Training,** starting from the Chairman and the BT Management Board, this training has been 'cascaded' down through senior management to all other management teams. The purpose of these Workshops was to develop an understanding of the mission, strengths and weaknesses of the organisation, and the techniques and objectives of Total Quality Management. This has led to a high degree of commitment to the programme by management. Three of the top five management levels have now completed this training process. Although the managers themselves run the workshops, they are assisted by full-time Implementation Support Managers, Facilitators and Trainers.

o **Quality Improvement Team Training,** in 'tools and techniques', based on a wide range of technical features, in which the portfolio is constantly under review. The aim is for all Quality Improvement Team members to have this training before starting their Projects.

The workshop-based programme is aimed at all 37,000 managers within the organisation, and is now three-quarters of the way towards completion. Following their workshop training, all managers are encouraged to set up a quality improvement programme of their own, with a suitably chosen team. Approximately 25 per cent of managers who have been through the programme now have quality projects in their own areas. The aim is for these projects to become a normal and continuous part of business activity.

In 1986, when TQM was launched, there was a slow build-up of this training and quality improvement process, but three years later the 'cascade' has 'really got going'. In the first six months of 1989, the number of managers going through the workshops and initiating projects has doubled.

Once all 37,000 managers have been trained and are working along these lines, the training programme will be rolled out to the remaining 200,000 people in the organisation. In some districts this process has already been started on a pilot basis, with one or two day workshops for office and engineering staffs.

HOW THE SYSTEM WORKS

The Quality Improvement Teams (QITs) set up by managers who have been through the training programme consist of seven or eight members, looking at an issue or problem central to their own and the manager's work. The choice of team members is dictated entirely by the skills and experience required, irrespective of rank or professional discipline. Many project teams, therefore, include office and engineering staff who have not received the management workshop training, although they do receive specialised training in Tools and Techniques. Membership of a team is entirely voluntary.

Quality Councils

Quality Councils, which have been set up at all levels of the organisation (Group, Departmental, Business Unit and District), approve, monitor and 'sign off' completed projects. These Quality Councils meet once every one or two months according to their size and the amount of activity. A national data base has been set up for Quality Improvement Projects which provides information on all projects in place or completed.

Quality Action Teams

In addition to the QITs, Quality Action Teams (QATs) are now being set up which operate on a work unit basis. As such they resemble quality circles, being smaller than most Quality Improvement Teams and meeting on a more regular basis. These teams might spend time each week assessing their current level of performance as a unit, and deciding how it could be improved. The emphasis in these teams is on their solving problems and implementing change on areas where they have the most impact. The Quality Action Team structure is seen as a way of accelerating the roll-out process beyond management level.

TQM AND WORKING TIME

The widespread programme of quality improvement being implemented within BT is having an increasing impact on working time, and the allocation of time between day-to-day work and the demands of the quality improvement programme has undoubtedly created pressure on existing priorities. However, BT's Group Director of Quality sees this conflict lessening as the quality culture eventually merges with 'business as usual'. The effort now being put into asserting the importance of quality is justified as 'ultimately building a better machine rather than spending time fixing the one we've got'.

For managers, the new approach offers an opportunity to get away from the familiar atmosphere of crisis management towards a strategic management style that works on planning and prevention rather than 'fixing' failures. Eventually, therefore, it will make more effective use of everyone's time.

At senior management level, up to 20 per cent of working time is now likely to be spent on working with teams, on training and in pursuing corporate quality goals. For some quality 'gurus', who advocate 30-40 per cent of senior management time, this is a relatively small proportion.

Below senior management level, among for example sales, materials distribution and accounts management staff, the amount of working time spent on quality might typically be between five and 10 per cent. Non-managerial employees are likely to spend a much smaller proportion of their time on the programme. For example, a telephone engineer who had spent ten years dealing with customer faults might need to give up one day a month to contribute to a project team (though not all such employees would be called upon). However, many employees at this level have an enormous store of experience of immense potential value to the organisation, and their widespread participation in projects is seen as helping significantly to reinforce a changed culture in which quality improvement becomes everyone's responsibility. This particularly applies to frontline staff who deal directly with customers.

COMMUNICATING TOTAL QUALITY MANAGEMENT

Communications within and between all levels of the workforce are seen as crucial in changing the culture of the organisation. The Awareness Training Programme, which has now reached all employees, has already played an important part in putting across basic quality improvement techniques, but communicating a changed set of goals and the elements of the new corporate culture is more difficult.

In order to achieve this, each division within the organisation is required to develop a communications programme, which is monitored at top management level. Managers then develop a communications strategy within this structure, with targets and goals. Within the biggest unit, British Telecom UK, an Employee Communications Manager has been appointed at senior level. This manager now runs a communications unit as part of the business division's aim of developing an overall communications strategy.

Team Briefings

Part of the communications strategy consists of Team Briefings, which are becoming widespread within the organisation. These are seen as a two-way process rather than just simply 'dumping' information on employees. Within the Team Briefing structure, a core brief is formulated at management board level, plus each of the 29 districts which each has its own management board. This is then conveyed to the local management team and 'cascaded' down the line to all employees. The core brief can be connected to Group, Divisional or local issues, or to a corporate promotion such as the recent 'Whicker's World', a set of four, fifteen-minute videos showing how BT compares with its global competitors. These are being used as a basis for monthly discussions at local level, led by management followed by first-line supervision. No issue is buried at Team Briefing sessions - if a question is not currently relevant, it will be raised at a later date, and if it cannot be answered on the spot, it is investigated so that an answer can be provided.

Other Consultation and Motivation Methods

The equivalent of quality circles within British Telecom are called Quality Action Teams. These have been set up in a small number of Districts and are in the pilot stage, but are intended to extend throughout the organisation. Other ways of consulting and motivating the workforce, include BT's long-standing suggestion scheme, which has now been revamped under the title 'New Ideas 88'. This awards cash prizes for suggestions, with an emphasis on those which save money. The organisation is now considering a National Quality Award Scheme for outstanding achievement in quality and service to customers. This would extend to local quality award schemes.

The relaunch of the suggestion scheme has produced many more ideas, running into thousands. The backing and commitment of the local management boards, in addition to the higher value of the awards and generally better organisation of the scheme, have contributed to this. A special unit has now been set up to administer the suggestions.

BT aims to gain consistent employee response. Consultants have been brought in to assist in setting up regular employee surveys, and the results have shown definite signs that the employee response to the Total Quality programmes is becoming positive. One or two joint employee/consumer working groups have also been set up, but this approach has not yet been adopted widely within the programme. The company has held meetings on quality with its suppliers and is carrying out joint quality improvement projects with some of them.

IMPACT ON EMPLOYEES

As yet there is no strong linkage between TQM and changes in terms and conditions. Total Quality is seen not as a set of additional responsibilities, but as the way business is done in BT. However, BT's Director of Quality commented that once the quality perspective has permeated the organisation, it will have a considerable influence on the industrial relations environment within the company.

'Repatterning'

Along with the major focus on training resulting from the quality perspective goes a parallel concern with changing patterns of work. Flexible work organisation ('repatterning') has recently been negotiated with the trade unions in order to break down traditional barriers between different areas of work. Previously, for example, if an internal faults engineer was called to a customer's home and diagnosed an external fault, a second engineer would be brought in to deal with it. 'Repatterning', which was tied in with a pay increase, has broken down many of these traditional demarcations and means that employees will take on a wider, more flexible range of work.

Also, different professional grades can now work in a single supervisory unit, whereas before they worked largely in their own professional heirarchies. Although these changes have not been linked to the formal TQM programme, their implications clearly relate to focusing on customer service and the company's quality goals.

Performance-related Pay

Performance-related pay was introduced three or four years ago for all managers. At the time the system was not introduced as a quality improvement measure, although it clearly related to the competitive environment. Annual increments for managers are now no longer automatic, but are subject to satisfactory performance. They can therefore be withheld when performance is particularly poor. Individually-tailored bonus packages have now also been introduced for the top 25 per cent of managers. These can provide up to 10-15 per cent of salary for performance measured against a set of personal objectives which include a quality component.

The performance-related pay scheme is based on a system of performance appraisal and counselling which goes back to BT's days as a Civil Service department. There is now an explicit attempt to link this system with quality and the overall values of the company.

TRADE UNION RESPONSE

The trade unions have been kept fully informed throughout the introduction of BT's Total Quality Programme, and in some cases union representatives have been given separate workshop training by the company. The unions' general response to the programme has been positive. However, there have been some specific concerns expressed by the Society of Telecommunications Executives, BT's management union, about the application of personal objectives and other forms of individualised pay packages to its members.

In a wider context some suspicions remain among the unions - for example that TQM is a way of bypassing and undermining trade union organisation, and that personal objectives and individual contracts of employment for managers cut across national agreements negotiated with the unions. For these reasons, while there is a high level of co-operation in many parts of the organisation, there is still a lack of full partnership between management and unions on the changes required for BT to become a quality organisation.

INTRODUCING THE CORPORATE CULTURE

BT's mission statement and its core values on which the new corporate culture is based, have been widely circulated within BT, for example on a small plastic card issued to most managers. BT values are aimed at putting across the message to British Telecom's employees that quality is everybody's concern. They are not intended as a set of 'pious statements' but are the basis for framing operational programmes. A system of monitoring their application is being set up.

COST IMPLICATIONS AND MEASURES OF SUCCESS

The cost of the TQM programme as a whole has been estimated at over £15m pa. This includes the use of hotels, training consultants and those employed full-time on the programme, but does not take into account the amount of working time given up by BT employees to the programme.

Against this expenditure can be weighed the savings which will be achieved by the 2,000 Quality Improvement Team projects now in the pipeline. On the 200 Projects already completed, £250,000 in savings has already been achieved, with a further £2m predicted. However, many current projects are indicating high potential savings and there is little doubt that the programme's benefits, both financial and service-related, will quickly outweigh the expenditure.

However, the ultimate test of the success of the programme will be whether BT meets the requirements of its customers and sustains growth in earnings for its shareholders. Although the programme is not about cost reduction, a reduction in the costs of failure is one of its targets, and BT has no doubt that these could yield substantial benefits. If estimates based on experience of other companies (commonly 20-25 per cent of expenditure) is taken as a guide, BT's estimated cost of failure or poor quality could be £1bn-2.5bn per annum. However, a substantial reduction in this area requires not just modification and improvement to the present systems and procedures, but a degree of basic reorganisation of business processes, and a deep commitment to the new culture. These targets will not be quickly or easily achieved, and BT's Chairman has emphasised that the company is engaged 'in a marathon, and not a sprint'.

MBS SERVICES

MBS Services provides a range of services to computer users, including maintenance and repair of equipment, education and training, and the design and installation of communications systems. The company employs 400 staff in various locations, including: 110 field engineers (going out to customer sites); 40 installation staff; 30 workshop engineers; 30 Customer Services Unit staff, including technical support engineers, contract staff and call schedulers (all dealing with customers by telephone); 12 credit control and commercial services staff; 25 education and training staff; and three sales staff. These staff add up to about 250, the balance of the 400 being provided by personnel, managerial, secretarial and switchboard staff. Management accounts for approximately 85 of these.

BACKGROUND

The company's Customer Care programme, which has been fully operational since the beginning of 1989, has two main strands. The first of these is the attempt to get the company accredited by the British Standards Institute (BS 5750), an increasingly prestigious mark of quality assurance. Obtaining the standard involves attaining quality standards in every aspect of the company's operations, including its job descriptions. One branch of MBS in Hull has now obtained BS5750 and this is seen as a spur for the whole company. A Quality Administrator was appointed in order to deal with the British Standards project and, following this, a Quality Manager was brought in to co-ordinate company policy on quality as a whole.

A staff development and education programme, entitled 'Who Cares Wins', is the second strand of quality development. It is hoped that all employees who have contact with the customer will have been through this programme by the end of the year, and eventually it will apply to all staff throughout the company.

The 'Who Cares Wins' programme had already been tried the previous year but had been shelved because there was no specific personnel input. It was made a personnel responsibility from 1 January 1989 and from this date the company was also restructured to align the personnel function with MBS Services line operations, in contrast to the corporate personnel function previously exercised by the whole group.

MBS has now incorporated the quality issue within its 'mission statement', which has been included in its annual reports since 1985 and is changed yearly. The current statement pledges that: 'We Maximise The Benefits Of

Our Customers' Information Systems By Providing The Best Services Available'.

Why The Company Introduced Customer Care

The overall rationale for seeking BS5750 and introducing the 'Who Cares Wins' programme also stems from two sources. The first of these was the recognition, some two years ago, that customer service would be the 'thing of the future' - this stemmed from the company's new Managing Director, previously with IBM, who took a long-term view in which MBS was to be developed as a quality service company.

Secondly, in order to expand its awareness of customer requirements, the company took on external consultants who recommended the 'Who Cares Wins' programme. MBS had previously used only customer satisfaction questionnaires to monitor the quality of its services.

The 'Who Cares Wins' programme had already been effectively used by the Austin Rover organisation to promote customer care within its dealerships. The new emphasis on quality and customer service is part of a strategic awareness by MBS of the need to keep ahead in the very competitive field in which it operates.

CUSTOMER CARE IN PRACTICE

At present a major priority within MBS is the achievement of BS5750 and, as a result, the company is concentrating on writing a dual quality and operations manual as required under the standard. Each department is therefore being surveyed in order to obtain a detailed breakdown of quality levels within different operations.

Major restructuring of the company had already taken place just prior to the introduction of the customer care programme. However, this restructuring was itself based on the increased awareness of the need to improve and monitor quality. A year previously MBS was 'not a quality company' and there were no management reports on the quality of service provision out in the field. Now, as a 'basic commercial necessity', the company has restructured on the basis of setting up quality groups in each operating unit, with a quality monitoring employee as the centre of each group. These employees, who are taken from the level of technical support management, have now been moved into a central logistical unit which main priority is the monitoring of quality within the organisation. So far, the major impact of the quality monitoring process has been in the engineering workshop, which has installed better environmental services aimed at improving quality.

PERSONNEL IMPLICATIONS

The twin-track approach of the company to customer service, centred on BS5750 and 'Who Cares Wins', has meant raising employee awareness on two fronts. Regarding attainment of BS5750, a 'general consciousness raising' has taken place in which all employees are now aware of the existence of a central quality team and of the visits which this team is making to all departments.

The 'consciousness raising' on BS5750 has been carried out via memos to employees and articles in the in-house magazine. As part of this initial stage of improved quality awareness the customer satisfaction questionnaire has been revamped and 'resurrected' on the basis that engineers who gain good customer feedback may receive 'excellence' awards consisting for example of a complimentary meal for two.

The 'Who Cares Wins' programme, as a more recent innovation, is about to start its second phase. Two employees have been selected from each of MBS' four regions to help in the implementation of the programme; one of these will act as a contact point for all employees, and both will be involved in training. Each region has further selected a list of employees for phased involvement in the project. Control clerks, who schedule service calls, and other customer service staff were initially targeted rather than engineers on site, who will be involved in the next phase.

For each of the regions, this amounts to a group of roughly 30, who are then subdivided into groups of between six and eight employees. These groups then take part in a series of 'Who Cares Wins' workshops, which consist typically of four afternoons spread over a twelve-week period. The workshops consist of a video-led discussion session, linked to a workbook, so that participants deal with two videos and two workbooks during the programme. The videos are based on the Austin Rover version of the 'Who Cares Wins' programme, but the workbooks have been tailored along MBS lines.

Those managers involved in training have themselves been given prior counselling by external consultants who provided a 'Train the Trainers' session. The Personnel Manager hopes to hold 'Who Cares Wins' team meetings after the workshops in which management can obtain some response. The managers concerned are currently liaising on how the next sessions will be organised: for example the training manager may carry out three sessions while the project manager or 'contact point' supervises only one.

Employee Attitudes And Practices

Employee attitudes are not seen as a problem at MBS, where the workforce is said by management to be 'very professional'. It says that employees recognise that their careers and livelihoods depend on customer awareness. As the Personnel Manager commented: 'We're only earning money when everyone out there is satisfying the customer'.

Some employees are less likely to see the need for this approach when their job involves limited or no contact with customers, but even these people have not put up barriers to the policy and have been rapidly convinced of its value.

Consultation And Motivation Of Workforce

The company sees its internal communications as 'our single biggest weakness'. The main obstacle is the wide disparity in job functions and geographical location throughout the company. A top management decision has now been taken to cascade communications down throughout the company, but a major problem is that the field engineers are never on site. To overcome this problem, important items for communication may now be enclosed in their pay slips.

The company publishes an in-house magazine which, following a rather fallow period, has recently been revamped and relaunched. Problems with communication were revealed via a recent employee attitude survey which revealed that most people heard things after the event, through the grapevine or not at all. The survey itself was the first undertaken within the company, but it is now intended to carry out such surveys as often as is appropriate. As a 'morale indicator' each survey will be compared with the previous year, to audit progress.

A major problem for the company in instituting better communications has so far been time, but now that a central quality team has been established it is hoped that the many suggestions for dealing with the problem can now be put into practice.

Pay And Conditions Issues

All MBS employees are paid on a performance-related basis and this has been true since the foundation of the company some eight years ago. Annual appraisals are carried out and all increments are performance-related. There is no annual cost-of-living increase - good performance, promotion or applying for a higher grade job are the only options open to employees to increase their incomes. The performance-related pay system is based on a job-evaluated grading structure.

Assessment of performance is relatively straightforward in the case of field engineers, but this has recently been extended to include a customer satisfaction requirement and will ultimately contain detailed standard specifications on quality. Each engineer serves approximately 25 customers and a quality-related criterion on performance may now be built into the system. This may involve, for example, not losing more than one contract a year. The engineers should work in such a way as to build up loyalty among their customers.

Given the nature of the service, there are problems with linking pay more closely to productivity, since it is not possible to measure systematically the timing on a wide range of varied jobs. The service is linked to customer demand and it is the responsibility of the call schedulers, who allocate engineers to customers on a timetabled basis, to ensure that there is as little slack as possible in matching service to demand. The rare cases of an engineer failing to reach a customer as arranged are dealt with on an individual basis.

There are no trade unions within MBS and the workforce has never demanded recognition of a union. This is explained by the company in terms of its competitive salaries (aiming to be in the upper quartile), and the ability to offer 'one of the best employment packages' in the computer industry. This includes a company car where appropriate, non-contributory pension, BUPA, life assurance, 23 days' holiday, and 'share-save' (save-as-you-earn) schemes. The company is also planning to introduce profit sharing. The intention is to provide a top employment package within the industry, aimed principally at staff recruitment and retention.

THE COST OF CUSTOMER CARE

The company says that its customer care programme is not yet at a stage where success is quantifiable. While it is felt that 'Who Cares Wins' has already made a difference, no precise measurements of progress are made. However, the company is considering the matter. Customer satisfaction is the most likely factor to be used for measurement, and this may take the form of a more detailed customer satisfaction survey.

The policy is costed (by comparison with similar exercises carried out by other companies) at approximately £300,000, including the salary of the new Quality Manager. A major element in the cost is the loss of working days in order to allow engineers and other employees to take part in training. With 160 engineers each losing half a day, this is equivalent to 80 working days lost throughout the year. The company is considering asking people to undertake training outside working hours and is hoping to be able to persuade staff to agree to this.

It is hoped that the cost of the policy will be rapidly recouped through attracting more customers as the result of enhancing the company's reputation and hence sales. At present the number of customers not renewing their contracts remains static rather than falling as a result of the customer care policy, but this is seen as due to a different set of problems. The market in which MBS operates is extremely competitive and currently unstable, making the consistent projection and measurement of a customer care approach difficult. Even if 'Who Cares Wins' does not immediately increase the company's market share, it is seen as having given MBS 'more of a team feeling than ever before'.

A corporate culture for the organisation as a whole is the company's objective, but the company has not yet arrived at an agreed definition of this culture in terms of core values or other corporate statements. This is ascribed to the large number of major changes within the company over the past two years. A senior management meeting recently took place at which the issues of improving services and establishing a corporate culture were considered, the results of which will slowly permeate through the company. Important elements in the projection of a new customer-oriented image for the company will be its slogan, 'Team MBS' and the distinctive logo already used as part of the company's consistent corporate image.

BIBLIOGRAPHY

Books

Ron Collard **Total Quality: Success Through People** IPM 1989

W. Edwards Deming **Out Of The Crisis** Cambridge University Press 1986

Joseph M. Juran **Managerial Breakthrough** McGraw Hill, New York 1964

T. Peters and N. Austin **A Passion For Excellence: The Leadership Difference** Fontana 1985

T. Peters and B. Waterman **In Search Of Excellence** Harper and Row 1982

Articles

Syd Hall, "Introducing and Sustaining Organisational Development in a Local Authority", paper by **Blyth Valley Borough Council** Personnel and Management Services Officer, October 1987.

Robin Hambleton, "Consumerism, Decentralisation and Local Democracy", **Public Administration** Theme Issue on "Consumerism and Beyond", Vol 66 No. 2, Summer 1988

A. Hancox, L. Worrall and J. Pay "Developing a Customer Oriented Approach to Service Delivery: The Wrekin Approach" **Local Government Studies** Vol 15, No. 1, January/February 1989

Edmund Heery, "A Common Labour Movement? Left Labour Councils and Trade Unions" in **Decentralisation and Democracy** ed Paul Hoggett and Robin Hambleton, School for Advanced Urban Studies Occasional Paper 28, 1987

Labour Research "HRM - Human Resource Manipulation?" **Labour Research** August 1989

Jenny Potter, "Consumerism and The Public Sector", **Public Administration** Summer 1988

Tony Tiernan, "The man who taught the Japanese about quality management", **Works Management** May 1988

"Town Hall Ratings", Consumers' Association Survey, **Which?** March 1989

Other Publications

Association of Labour Authorities, Local Government Information Unit, London Strategic Policy Unit, and Association of Direct Labour Organisations, **Don't Panic**, 1988

British Standards Institute, **BS 5750/ISO 9000: 1987 - A Positive Contribution to Better Business** and **Quality Assurance: The Way To Capture New Markets**, available from BSI Quality Assurance, PO Box 375, Milton Keynes MK14 6LL

Corrigan, Jones, Lloyd and Young, **Socialism, Merit and Efficiency**, Fabian Society Pamphlet No. 530, September 1988

DHSS **Primary Health Care: An Agenda For Discussion** 1986 HMSO

Department of Health, **Working For Patients,** White Paper on the government's review of the NHS, HMSO Cmnd 555

Sir Roy Griffiths **An Enquiry into the Management of the NHS** Department of Health and Social Security 1983 HMSO

Joiner Association of Madison, Wisconsin, "A Practical Approach To Quality" of **Managing into the 90s: The Deming Philosophy,** Department of Trade and Industry December 1988

King's Fund Centre **Living well into old age: applying principles of good practice to services for people with dementia** King's Fund Publishing Office 1986

Labour Party, Labour Co-ordinating Committee **Go Local To Survive** 1984 (see Martin Smith p.17)

Labour Party occasional paper, **Quality Street,** May 1989

Labour Party Policy Review First Report, **Social Justice and Economic Efficiency** June 1988

Labour Party Policy Review Final Report, **Meet the challenge, Make the change,** June 1989

National Council for Voluntary Organisations **Clients' Rights: Report of an NCVO Working Party** Bedford Square Press 1984

National Consumer Council **Measuring Up: Consumer Assessment of Local Authority Services** NCC 1986

National Union of Public Employees **Better Services: A NUPE Handbook for Good Local Services** NUPE 1987

Martin Smith, **The Consumer Case For Socialism** Fabian Pamphlet No. 513, July 1986

John Stewart and Michael Clarke **Getting Closer To The Public** Local Government Training Board 1987

Craig Thomson **Client Satisfaction: Monitoring Quality** Coombe Lodge (Further Education Staff College) Report Special Volume 20 No. 12

Kieron Walsh "Quality and Competition" **Competition and Local Authorities** No. 4, Local Government Training Board August 1988

Wrekin Council **In Research Of Customers** available from the Personnel Unit, District of the Wrekin Council, PO Box 213, Malinslee House, Telford, Shropshire TF3 4LL